*Number Nineteen: The Centennial Series
of the Association of Former Students,
Texas A&M University*

THE FORGOTTEN CATTLE KING

The Forgotten Cattle King

By

BENTON R. WHITE

TEXAS A&M UNIVERSITY
College Station

Copyright © 1986 by Benton R. White
All rights reserved

Library of Congress Cataloging-in-Publication Data

White, Benton R. (Benton Ray), 1949–
  The forgotten cattle king.

  (Centennial series of the Association of Former Students,
Texas A&M University; no. 19)
  Bibliography: p.
  Includes index.
  1. Oxsheer, Fountain Goodlet, 1849–1931. 2. Ranchers—
Texas—Biography. I. Title. II. Series.
SF194.2.093W47 1986   338.7′6362′00924 [B]   85-40749
ISBN 0-89096-250-2 (cloth); 0-89096-998-1 (pbk.)

Manufactured in the United States of America
FIRST PAPERBACK EDITION

To the Memory of
Frances Beal Smith Hodges
and to my parents

In all branches of the livestock industry he was a "pioneer." His experiments in the breeding of better range cattle were as numerous as . . . the trails he blazed in West Texas.

> beneath the portrait of F. G. Oxsheer, "The Hall of Cattle Kings," Texas Centennial Exposition, 1936

Contents

List of Illustrations	xiii
List of Maps	xv
Acknowledgments	xvii
Prologue	3
1 The Trail from Ruin	7
2 Joys and Sorrows	19
3 The Awesome Plains	34
4 A Cattleman's Legacy	50
5 Revolutions	64
6 The Patriarch and His Flock	80
7 The Gamble of a Lifetime	97
8 Until the Last Dawn Breaks	108
Epilogue	121
Postscript	123
Appendix: F. G. Oxsheer Family	125
Selected Bibliography	127
Index	135

Illustrations

following page 18
William and Martha Oxsheer
F. G. Oxsheer
John Beal
Mary Oxsheer
F. G. Oxsheer
F. G. and Mary Oxsheer Wedding Portrait
F. G. and Mary's First Home
The Oxsheer Home, Colorado City
Cowhands on the Oxsheer Ranch
Windmill Remnant on the Oxsheer Ranch
Oxsheer Family Portrait
F. G., Jr. in Mexico
F. G., Jr., Ranch Superintendent
General Ledger Balance, Sainapuchic
F. G. and Mary on Vacation
The Oxsheer Mansion, Fort Worth
Portraits of F. G, Jr., Drennan, and Coke
The Diamond Ranch Outfit
A Cowhand at the Diamond Ranch
F. G. and Mary at Diamond Ranch Headquarters
F. G. Oxsheer's "Cotton Patch"
Diamond Ranch Letterhead
Dust Storm, Stanton, 1931
F. G. Oxsheer

Maps

Central Texas	8
The Chisholm Trail	14
The Trek West	32
Trail from the Pecos River	46
Llano Estacado	51
The Oxsheer Ranches	124

Acknowledgments

THIS work is a testament to the labor, kindness, and abilities of many people, particularly the chairman of my dissertation committee at Texas Christian University, Don Worcester. His in-depth knowledge of the range cattle industry as well as his extraordinary writing skills and ability to teach writing methods have served as a constant guide. To be told that my work reflects his writing style in any way is to be paid the highest compliment. There are others at TCU who have also offered insight and thought-provoking suggestions: Frank Reuter, Don Coerver, and Kathryne McDorman, as well as Ross Bush, and Jim Kettle, a graduate student and a gifted editor.

Also contributing their time and expertise were David J. Murrah and his staff at the Texas Tech Southwest Collection in Lubbock. They have a veritable gold mine of primary source materials on West Texas history, and I could not have asked for more professional or courteous assistance in my research. I am also indebted to the many individuals that I have interviewed. Hiley Boyd, Jr., of the Texas Tech Ranching Heritage Center spent hours recounting family stories of life on the open range and how his father worked for "Col. Fount Oxsheer." Edwyna Thro, a wonderful and gracious woman and a granddaughter of F. G. Oxsheer, supplied many personal anecdotes and intimate details. A note of thanks and recognition are due my father B. B. White and Robert N. Schultz, Anella Slaughter Bauer, Mrs. Bill West, and Robert Beal. Each of them contributed more than one good idea or useful piece of information. A special thank-you is also in order for a special person, Chris Schultz; without her many excellent suggestions and constant support this work would not have been completed.

The entire W. A. Oxsheer family of Fort Worth is due special recognition and thanks; they generously supplied me with the Oxsheer Family Papers as well as personal interviews. Without their help and information this work would have been impossible. Finally, and most important, I am indebted to someone I never met, Frances Hodges, the granddaughter of F. G. Oxsheer who grew up in his home. For twenty-seven years Mrs. Hodges compiled the Oxsheer Family Papers. Her memoirs of life with her grandfather are priceless, and I regret she did not live to see this work completed.

Researching and writing the history of F. G. Oxsheer has been a labor of love mixed with a certain amount of frustration, for parts of the record are hopelessly incomplete. He was a typical nineteenth-century cattleman and kept much of his business in his head instead of on paper. As a result, I suspect that I have underplayed the historical significance of this pioneer cattle baron and left some of the story untold. He probably owned ranches in Kansas and California in the early 1900s, for example, but the evidence is inconclusive, and I have omitted any reference to these holdings in the text. Other pitfalls in researching and writing might be mentioned, but I fear I have already gone on too long. F. G. Oxsheer was generally a man of few words, and I see no reason why his biographer should not learn from his example. Any errors or oversights in this work are strictly my own.

THE FORGOTTEN CATTLE KING

Prologue

It was nearly dark when the locomotive pulled into the little town of Stanton. Already lights shone from the coach-car windows, and the evening star sparkled in a red-orange western sky. Another day on the West Texas plains was ending. In the light of the depot stood a single figure—silent, motionless—staring at the train. His name was Fountain Goodlet Oxsheer, called simply "F. G." or "Fount." Tall and angular, with shoulders back and head up, he looked fit and vigorous at first glance, like a man in his prime. But a closer look at his weathered face, the sunken eyes, gray hair, and hearing horn told a different story. Wearing the finest of tailor-made suits and hand-fashioned boots, white collar and cuffs, silk tie and Stetson hat, he stood in the gathering gloom like a living monument to another time.[1]

The train had scarcely stopped when he walked slowly to the nearest car. For an instant he paused, then stepped inside. Normally he would have gone to a sleeping car, but this evening, for some unaccountable reason, he entered the day coach. Along the green-carpeted aisle he walked, past gentlemen in suits and coarse figures in sweat-stained overalls, chic ladies with bobbed hair, and leathery-looking women in bonnets, past bearded old men and squirming children. All these F. G. passed, scarcely noticing them.

Next he passed through the smoking car, where seated men talked, probably about Republicans, the depression, and the Democratic nominee Franklin D. Roosevelt, but F. G. could not hear them. He continued on to the next car, and then to another. Finally he opened a door and stepped out onto the platform at the end of the train. Alone and in silence, he gazed into the twilight.

In a few moments the car shook, and the train began to move. It crept by the little depot, then, gathering speed, moved past cattle pens and wooden shacks, a cotton gin, and vacant lots. In a matter of seconds the train was at the edge of town racing to the east. Wheels clattered on steel rails, and hot winds whipped into the face of the

---

[1] Frances Hodges, "Memoirs," in possession of the W. A. Oxsheer family, Fort Worth, Tex.

man standing on the platform. Another minute and Stanton was only a cluster of lights on the flat horizon.[2]

Off to the left F. G. saw other lights a few miles away. They marked his Diamond Ranch, all that was left of a lifetime of labor. Not much of a show—ten thousand mortgaged acres and a few hundred head of cattle, a pitiful remnant of a ranching empire that had once made him a virtual monarch.[3]

How things had changed. Once his ranching domain was larger than some Eastern states or European nations. Eighteen ranches had carried the Oxsheer brands, eighteen large ranches scattered across the Southwest in a great arc from Oklahoma and West Texas south across the Rio Grande into Chihuahua. No cattleman ever controlled a more intricate ranching network. In the past, his cowhands had counted his stock by the tens of thousands.

He had started half a century ago, pushing a herd of longhorns onto the Texas South Plains, the last unsettled region of the state. Later he raised mainly purebred stock, and with his old friend C. C. Slaughter, changed the face of the American beef cattle industry, converting Texas from a land of rangy longhorns to the home of award-winning Herefords. So great was the reputation of his cattle, men throughout the West bought them sight unseen. In Mexico it was the same story: the introduction of purebred herds, then recognition as a leading cowman. American investors like Frank Rockefeller hung on his every word of advice. With W. T. Waggoner, another pioneer rancher, he also bred saddle horses from the finest stallions. It took good horseflesh, F. G. always said, to produce the best cow pony. He even imported a registered jack and jenny from Spain to upgrade his mule stock. En route from Europe, these animals had remained on exhibit for weeks at the 1899 Texas State Fair in Dallas.[4]

But all this was long past, nearly a lifetime ago, or so it seemed. Now he was old, tired, and sick with worry, hanging on to a fragment of what was left in a world he no longer understood. For months he had worked like a man half his age; for weeks he'd hardly slept. The worsening economic depression was continually on his mind. In his day they had been called "money panics," but whatever the name, the effect was the same: debts, mortgages, foreclosures, ruin. Worst of all, the son who bore his name and who could have stepped into his boots in this troubled time was gone. He had never recovered from the loss of his eldest son, though he had continued the struggle

[2] W. A. Oxsheer, interview with the author, Fort Worth, Tex., July 6 and 7, 1983.
[3] W. A. Oxsheer, interview.
[4] Hodges, "Memoirs"; Pamphlet of Mexican Hereford Breeding and Importing Company, n.d., Chillicothe, Mo., Oxsheer Family Papers, Fort Worth, Tex. Deed Records, vol. 15, p. 308, Haskell County Courthouse, Haskell, Tex.

to provide for his family's every need and desire. He would sit far into the night, circling his thumbs forward and backward, asking himself the same questions over and over: How could he save the ranch? What would become of his family if he failed? He had faced hard times and debts before, as well as a multitude of other calamities that had threatened to crush him. His whole life had been a struggle, but he had always triumphed. Now he was eighty-one, and there was no one left to whom he could turn for help or advice. He was the last of a special breed—the old-time Texas cattle baron.[5]

It was soon dark, and the ranch lights vanished over the horizon. For one last minute F. G. stared into the darkness, then turned, opened the coach-car door, and stepped inside. Noticing an empty seat to his left, he sat down, taking off his hat and placing it on the seat along with his hearing horn. He sighed, leaned back, and gazed out the window into the night. Maybe he had lived too long, seen too much. So much had changed. Slowly his eyes closed, and the swirl of worries were forgotten as he drifted off into his dreams—dreams about a land, a boy, a family, and a river—dreams of another place and another time.

[5] Edwyna Thro, interview with the author, Wichita Falls, Tex., May 30, 1983.

CHAPTER I

The Trail from Ruin

THEY came riding over the southwestern horizon—half a dozen in all. They rode down the hill to Little River, splashed across to the other side, then dripping wet, dashed up the bank. For a mile or more they followed the stream, their mustangs never breaking stride. Finally they turned from the river near a grove of post oaks, crossed bottomland and fields, and rode straight for a house on the bluff. Most of them had on homespun shirts, checked or butternut-colored pants tucked in boots, and remnants of Confederate uniforms. All wore dark broad-brimmed hats or Mexican sombreros. At a distance the riders looked hardened and experienced, but as they trotted up, spurs jingling, their faces finally gave them away. The oldest was scarcely nineteen.[1]

Standing on the front porch waiting for them was F. G. Oxsheer. Tall, sandy-headed, he was only nineteen years old himself, but already the head of his household—a household facing ruin. His father, William, was still alive, but an accident at a cotton gin had left one hand permanently mangled, and he would never work his fields again. Martha, his mother, was sick in bed. No one knew how serious it was; there was no money for a doctor. The two sisters were mere children. A few former slaves remained: Miles, Emma, and one or two others, but the rest had scattered at the end of the war when Federal troops arrived in Cameron. Fields were weed choked, fences down, and bands of renegades roamed the country, stealing, plundering, and killing. Men carried guns wherever they went, and each slept with one beside his bed. Hoofbeats in the night could mean friends or neighbors, or they might mean bandits.[2]

[1] Description of the terrain is based on author's tour of Little River bottom. Robert Beal, interview with the author, Fort Worth, Tex., June 30, 1983.
[2] Frances Hodges, "Memoirs," in possession of the W. A. Oxsheer family, Fort Worth, Tex. John Drennan Oxsheer to Frances Hodges, Nov. 24, 1957, and Oct. 24,

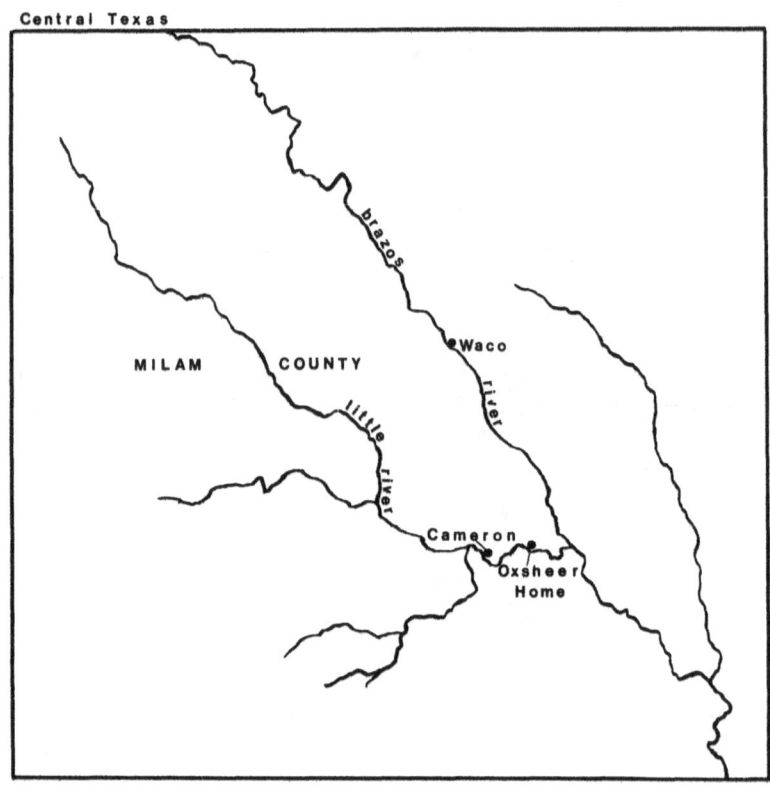
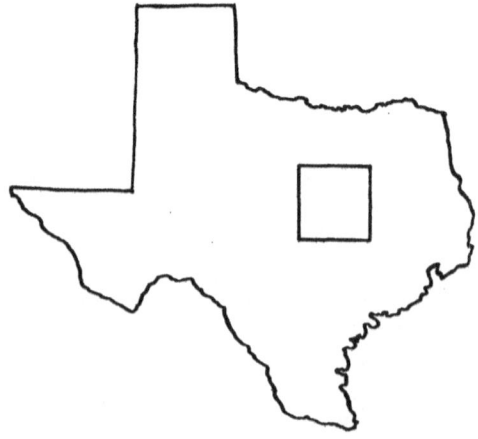

There was no one to turn to for protection or help. What passed for government and law was called Reconstruction, but to F. G. it looked more like a mixture of chaos and tyranny. The U.S. Army had been empowered to remove or replace civil authorities at will. They carried out a purge, dismissing officeholders en masse, often replacing them with vicious incompetents. Anyone with a Confederate past, especially with a planter background like that of the Oxsheers, was fair game for this crowd. F. G. still smoldered when he recalled walking down the streets of Cameron with his father, past grinning, blue-clad troops and their political underlings—those strutting little bantam roosters backed by Federal bayonets. The slightest word might result in public humiliation; any gesture or expression of resentment could mean arrest. This was life in Milam County, Texas, 1868. If something were not done, and fast, the Oxsheers would soon be destitute. There was nothing to prevent it, nothing but this boy waiting on the porch and some cattle penned in a large stockade by the barn.[3]

As the men, or boys, rode up, F. G. stepped off the porch to greet them. He shook hands with the leader, then turned and walked toward the barn, everyone following on horseback. As they came near the corral of palisade logs, they could see the tips of horns above the fence. Inside were nearly a hundred Texas longhorns, rangy, long-legged critters F. G. had rounded up from the surrounding woods and hills. They were all that was left besides the land and a few horses. Renegades had stripped them of everything else: mules, hogs, chickens—everything.[4]

The men with F. G. worked for a neighboring family named Beal. Before the war the Beals had been among the largest cattle dealers and planters in Central Texas. In fact, they were some of the first Anglo ranchers in the state. As early as the 1830s they were raising cattle. In the forties and fifties old "Massa John" Beal came through the country every year, buying cattle from the Oxsheers and their neighbors, then driving them to coastal cities like Galveston or Indianola. When the war came, he supplied beef to Confederate forces in Louisiana, driving

---

1964, Oxsheer Family Papers, in possession of the W. A. Oxsheer family, Fort Worth Texas; Anella Slaughter Bauer, interview with the author, Dallas, Tex., Dec. 15, 1983.

[3] John Drennan Oxsheer to Frances Hodges, Nov. 24, 1957 and Oct. 24, 1964, Oxsheer Family Papers.

[4] John Drennan Oxsheer to Frances Hodges, Nov. 24, 1957, Oxsheer Family Papers; Hodges, "Memoirs."

stock through tangled forests and nearly impenetrable swamps. Now his cowhands were back, this time gathering cattle to trail north to Kansas.[5]

An Illinois cattle dealer named Joseph McCoy was urging Texans to bring steers to a Kansas railhead called Abilene. He had built pens and corrals, and he had a promise from the railroads to ship cattle from Abilene to Chicago where stockyards had opened. Best of all, McCoy also promised that northern cattle dealers would be there and pay in gold for the cattle they bought. For the Beals and the Oxsheers or anyone else with cattle to sell, Abilene offered an escape from the economic calamity of Reconstruction.

The men camped that night by the Oxsheers' corral and in the morning rode away with the cattle, down the bluff, across the river, and over the distant hill the way they had come. But when they left they had company; Fount Oxsheer rode with them. He was going "up the trail" to Abilene.[6]

It should have been expected. F. G. had lived all his life on a farm, but even as a little boy he disliked farm chores: pulling weeds, gathering eggs, hoeing and chopping cotton with his father and the slaves. But there was another more serious reason for trailing a herd to Abilene. Selling a hundred longhorns would support the family for a year, but then what? The price of cotton was collapsing, and there was no reason to hope the fields would ever turn a profit again. On the other hand, there was money in driving cattle to Kansas. The Oxsheers, the entire family, had nearly exhausted themselves carving a home from the Little River bottom. Some had lost their lives along the way. No amount of hardship was going to take it from them, F. G. swore. He was going up the trail to learn the cow business, and build a new and better life for himself and his family.[7]

Miles and Emma would look after his mother and sisters. His father would be all right. If there was anyone who could manage on his own it was his father, crippled hand or not. When he had first settled in Milam County, he was miles from his nearest neighbor. Renegades

---

[5] Robert Beal, interview; John Drennan Oxsheer to Frances Hodges, Nov. 24, 1957, and Oct. 24, 1964, Oxsheer Family Papers.

[6] Edwyna Thro, interview with the author, Wichita Falls, Tex., May 30, 1983.

[7] Hodges, "Memoirs."

would probably leave them alone; there was nothing left to steal. Besides, F. G. assured himself, he would be back in a few months.[8]

It was hard to say good-bye. F. G. had never been away from his family, but it was the only way he could help them now. Maybe the last thing they did together was kneel in prayer; camp meetings and thundering sermons by frock-tailed circuit riders had always been a part of their lives. Theirs was a primitive faith, but also one of hope. Did God not cause his Chosen People to languish in captivity, to suffer under the heel of Ashur, Amon, and Baal before delivering them from bondage? If a family fell before sickness, war, debt, and poverty in these times then was there not hope? The Oxsheers believed in order to endure. It was all they had.[9]

For several days they rode, F. G. and the others, gathering more cattle. It was a familiar scene at every farm: gaunt, pitiful people, whipped by war and poverty, desperately hoping their cattle might save them. But at last, one morning they rode over a grassy hill and saw the big herd assembled for Abilene, nearly two thousand milling, bawling Texas longhorns. F. G. had never seen so many cattle. Several riders worked at one end of the great herd, cutting out and roping steers for "road branding" to designate ownership of cattle on the trail. Other men on the ground handled the hot irons that filled the air with the stench of burning hair.[10]

A dozen riders were heading up the trail, along with the trail boss, cook, and wrangler. Most of them were wiry little fellows. The wrangler who looked after the horses was just a boy, maybe fourteen years old, and took more than his share of kidding from the rest. An entire crew of experienced men was needed, but that was impossible; there was always a shortage of "top hands." Three or four in the outfit had trail experience; the rest were gangling farm boys—excited, and if the truth be known, a little frightened of what lay ahead—hoping the stories of Abilene and gold were true. Most had never been more than a day's ride from home.

---

[8] Anella Slaughter Bauer, interview; Hodges, "Memoirs"; Newspaper clipping, Oxsheer Family Papers. (This article relates an interview with William Oxsheer when he was an old man, and recounts his early years in Milam County.)

[9] Hodges, "Memoirs"; Edwyna Thro, interview.

[10] Robert Beal, interview.

Two brothers, John and Nick Beal, ran the outfit. Their father, "Massa John," was too old now for this kind of work. Nick, like F. G., was tall and lean. John, the trail boss, was the opposite. Broad-shouldered and bearded, he looked like his father and seemed older than the others though he wasn't. The boys looked up to John and carried out his orders promptly, but at the same time he was one of them. Everyone called him by his first name. He dipped his beans from the same pot, slept on the same ground, and never held himself above the rest. There was something else about him, a nervous habit really. In camp or on the trail, from the time he got up until he went to sleep, John talked endlessly. About cattle, the weather, men or women, rusty nails or banjo picks, about anything or nothing, he jabbered. No one was ever lonely when the boss was in camp; John could "talk the horns off a goat."[11]

When the spring grass was deep enough to furnish pasture, the men and the herd pulled out for Abilene. They followed the Chisholm Trail: six hundred miles from Central Texas north through the settlements of Waco and Fort Worth, then on to Indian Territory, and finally Kansas. For two or three months they would live in the saddle, eighteen hours at a time. The country was rolling and grassy, no fences or farms, just sky and prairie and two thousand Texas longhorns strung out for a mile or more.[12]

The two most experienced trail hands rode "point" on opposite sides of the lead steers, following the direction pointed out by John. Some distance behind on each side of the herd, other men rode "swing," and still farther back "flank" riders kept the moving column strung out. There was no shouting, whistling, or waving of arms. Anyone who did such a thing would have been booted out for trying to set off a stampede. Bringing up the rear were two or three hands riding "drag," nudging along sluggish or footsore animals. It was the dirtiest job of all and went to the greenest men. The cattle pulverized the ground as

---

[11] There are several contradictions concerning Beal genealogy. Some records list "Massa" John Beal as the grandfather rather than the father of John and Nick. Nick Beal's age is also uncertain; he may have been born as late as 1860 rather than 1850, the date noted in the Oxsheer Family Bible. If so, Nick was not on the Chisholm Trail with F. G. Oxsheer in 1868. But the evidence—a family Bible, memoirs, and personal interviews—suggests that events and family relations were as I have depicted in the narrative. Hodges, "Memoirs"; Family Bible, Oxsheer Family Papers; Robert Beal, interview.

[12] Hiley Boyd, Jr., interview with the author, Lubbock, Tex., June 13, 1983.

they passed, covering drag riders with a constant dust cloud. It wasn't the prettiest sight in the world either, dust and the rumps of longhorn steers, all day long. Every evening drag riders came in from the herd with a dust coating on eyebrows "thick as fur."[13]

The first few days they pushed the cattle hard, removing them from their home range as quickly as possible. If not, a few especially wild steers might break from the herd and race back. This was also a time to get a measure of the men. Greenhorns like F. G. learned as much about trailing cattle that first week as in the next two months combined.

After a week or two the cattle were trail broken, and everyone settled into a routine. Soon F. G. resembled just another cowhand, tanned and hardened to the trail. He learned what it meant to handle half-broken horses and to keep steers moving together without allowing any to trot off fat or to stray. He often wondered about his family as he rode along, hoping they were safe, but mostly he kept his mind on his work. As the days slipped into weeks, the kid from Milam County became a Texas drover.[14]

Late every afternoon the men pulled the herd off the trail at the bed ground John had selected. Two riders remained with the herd while the others rode to the chuckwagon and camp. With twilight the cattle began to lie down, and the riders forming the first watch circled slowly around them in opposite directions, singing old frontier lullabies. The only other sounds were yipping coyotes in the distance, the hooting of owls, or the grunts of cattle belching up their cuds. Through the night men guarded the herd in two-hour shifts, the first until ten o'clock, when one rider went in to wake up the next watch. Usually the cattle lumbered to their feet sometime in the night, stretched for a few minutes, then lay down to sleep until dawn. All of his life F. G. Oxsheer would speak of those nights with the herd, when he told time by the Big Dipper and followed the North Star to Kansas.[15]

It was a time for thinking—and remembering. Most of the boys had never known any other life but dog-run cabins, hoecakes, a corn patch, and a mule, but F. G. had grown up in a world of house servants and private tutors. Once the family had been one of the wealthiest in

---

[13] Hiley Boyd, Jr., interview; Robert Beal, interview.
[14] Hodges, "Memoirs."
[15] Hodges, "Memoirs"; Hiley Boyd, Jr., interview.

The Chisholm Trail

Milam County: two thousand acres in cotton, dozens of slaves, hundreds of horses, mules, and cattle. Wherever he went with his father, ladies curtsied and men bowed or sought advice on business and politics from "Colonel Oxsheer." They were less than fifty miles from the frontier, but their life resembled more than anything the Virginia gentry. The courtly manners, the social graces—it all seemed so strange and out of place now, like something that had never happened—but it was still a part of him. Life had been hard for the last several years, a struggle just to survive. But he still remembered the good times before the war: horse racing in Cameron, fishing on Little River, possum hunting in the woods with his dad and someone else, his little brother Willie.[16]

He and Willie were inseparable in those days. As close, he supposed, as brothers could be. But once when they were hauling a loaded wagon, Willie fell beneath the wheels and was crushed to death before F. G. could stop the team. It was a memory that had haunted F. G. ever since. No one blamed him. It was an accident, they said; it couldn't be helped. But that didn't matter. He could never really put it from his mind. Maybe that was part of the reason he was on the cattle trails. He was determined that his loved ones would never suffer again.[17]

At four o'clock the last shift came out to the herd and rode until dawn. Everyone else slept until, at the first hint of light, the entire crew was roused by the booming voice of the cook announcing breakfast and the start of another day on the trail.

By the time they crossed the Red River into Indian Territory, it was late April, the rainy season. Sometimes rainstorms battered the trail for days. The prairie turned into a bog, making the grass so poor that ponies grew weak and cattle lost weight. The trail became a quagmire, and every creek and river a raging torrent. Riders stayed with the herd, rain beating against their long yellow slickers and pouring off their wide-brimmed hats. The cook served half-raw and soggy food while men, soaked to the skin, simply endured. No one slept in a dry

---

[16] Hodges, "Memoirs"; Anella Slaughter Bauer, interview; John Drennan Oxsheer to Frances Hodges, Nov. 24, 1957, Oxsheer Family Papers.

[17] John Drennan Oxsheer to Frances Hodges, Nov. 24, 1957, Oxsheer Family Papers.

bed. Later F. G. believed that his hearing loss was the result of those rainy nights when he slept on the cold, wet ground.[18]

Early summer and the herd was in Kansas, but the trail was far to the west of most settlements. Only in the isolated town of Abilene were drovers and their cattle welcome. Everyone had heard of other trail drives that had ended in disaster when cowboys tried to move their cattle across settled land in eastern Kansas and western Missouri. Homesteaders correctly associated Texas longhorns with "Texas fever," a fatal disease transmitted by ticks. Northern cattle had no immunity. Bands of armed men had met these herds at the Kansas-Missouri borders and refused to let the Texas cattle pass. Several drovers had been beaten or killed, and their cattle stampeded. A few small herds were killed to the last animal.[19]

For a week or two, F. G. and the others moved along. Not until they were nearing Abilene did they meet an occasional family of homesteaders, and even then there were no incidents. F. G. was a little surprised when he saw them for the first time. They didn't look at all like he had imagined: no horns, pitchforks, or pointed tails, just ordinary folks. But some of the boys who had fought in the war didn't agree. Kansas sodbusters, they said, were nothing but Yankees come west. Most of the women and children were as "ugly as lye soap" they swore, and all of them had "necks like gourd handles." F. G. smiled, but said nothing. He had been too young to fight in the war. Till now the only Yankees he had ever seen were those in Cameron, and he didn't remember a thing about their necks.[20]

A day's drive from Abilene, they moved off the trail and called a halt, so the cattle could fatten on the rich prairie grass until the herd was sold. John Beal went into Abilene looking for buyers. Pairs of riders took shifts with the cattle. Everyone else hunted, gathered wild fruit, played cards or simply stretched out in the shade of the chuckwagon to get some sleep. It was their first chance for plenty of rest since they had left home. Between night herding and trailing cattle they had been lucky to get four or five hours of sleep at a time.[21]

In a few days John returned. It was true, he told them, Yankees

[18] Robert Beal, interview; Hiley Boyd, Jr., interview; Hodges, "Memoirs."
[19] Hiley Boyd, Jr., interview.
[20] Robert Beal, interview; Hiley Boyd, Jr., interview; Hodges, "Memoirs."
[21] Hiley Boyd, Jr., interview; Robert Beal, interview.

paid gold for Texas longhorns. He'd sold the herd. The cook hitched up the team while the men saddled their mounts, then strung out the steers for the last time and headed for the railway loading pens near the edge of Abilene. It was the end of the trail. Now the boys turned their thoughts to a night on the town.[22]

Abilene was famous—or infamous—all over the West. More than just a shipping point for cattle, it was a wild, sordid place, full of transients eager to separate trail hands from their pay. Cowboys talked of little else the last days on the trail but seeing "Texas Street," a collection of saloons, gambling dens, dancehalls, a few general stores and restaurants, and more saloons. Through the late 1800s a number of peace officers tried but failed to establish law and order. Some were killed; others simply quit or were run off by rowdy trail hands. When the citizens began building a stone jail, Texas drovers cheerfully tore it down.

But for every Texas cowhand who roared into Abilene to refight the Civil War or tear down the town, there was another like F. G. Oxsheer. He seldom drank, wouldn't have touched a deck of cards, and shunned the brothels. The old upbringing was too strong. For F. G., Abilene meant cattle sales, a bath, a haircut, and new clothes. It had been a long time since he had bought factory clothes. Since the war he'd worn nothing but homespun. Later he joined the others for a meal in town, and maybe a beer or two. He was usually with them wherever they went, but he took no part in their antics. In fact, he used his influence to keep his friends out of trouble. He seemed to be the one that others instinctively turned to for help, to get them to a hotel or back to camp if they were drunk or if someone pulled a gun. F. G. was quiet, almost timid in a crowd. But he had the respect of nearly everyone who knew him, even those who were older and more experienced, or who didn't share his code of ethics. He was only nineteen, but when he spoke, men listened.[23]

After a day or two most of the men were penniless, three months' pay spent with nothing left to show for their work but hangovers. Fuzzy headed, they saddled up and returned to camp, one or two heaving up last night's supper as they rode away. At camp they picked up the

---

[22] Hiley Boyd, Jr., interview; Robert Beal, interview.
[23] Edwyna Thro, interview; Hodges, "Memoirs."

wagon, the wrangler, and the *remuda*, then started on the long ride back to Texas. But not everyone was sick or broke. John and Nick Beal still had their money; so did F. G. Oxsheer. Now he could finance repairs on the family estate and put things in working order again. The old plantation would never be what it had been—the Civil War and collapse of cotton prices had seen to that. But he could at least save the land, see that his family had a roof over them, and know they would not starve. Maybe he could also buy more cattle in Texas, trail them north again, and make even more money. With a little luck and a lot of hard work maybe. . . . Well, who could say?[24]

As he rode south with the others, thinking back on his first long drive, F. G. was proud. He had a right to be. He also felt he had gained something in the way of a practical education. The hardships and dangers he had faced, the storms and swollen rivers, the many examples of grit and nerve he had witnessed, all had served to mature him. When he left home he was little more than a boy fighting to save his family and their land. He returned a cowboy, determined to become a Texas cattleman.[25]

[24] Hiley Boyd, Jr., interview; Hodges, "Memoirs."
[25] Hodges, "Memoirs."

William and Martha Oxsheer, the parents of Fountain Goodlet Oxsheer. (Oxsheer Family Papers)

Left, F. G. Oxsheer as a young man. *Right*, John Beal, the neighbor, early business partner, and then brother-in-law of F. G. Oxsheer. (Oxsheer Family Papers)

Left, Mary Beal Oxsheer, wife of F. G. Oxsheer. *Right*, F. G. Oxsheer. (Oxsheer Family Papers)

Left, the wedding portrait of F. G. and Mary Oxsheer. *Right*, F. G. and Mary Oxsheer's first home, situated on the bottomlands of the Little River. (Oxsheer Family Papers)

The Oxsheer home in Colorado City. (Oxsheer Family Papers)

Cowhands on the Oxsheer ranch. (Oxsheer Family Papers)

A remnant of a windmill on the old Oxsheer ranch. (Photograph by the author)

The Oxsheer family: (*front row*) F. G. holding Drennan, Coke, Mary, and F. G., Jr. (*Back row*) Mabel, Beal, and Myrtle. (Oxsheer Family Papers)

F. G., Jr. (*right*) in Mexico. (Oxsheer Family Papers)

F. G., Jr., during his tenure as superintendent of the Sainapuchic ranch in Mexico. (Oxsheer Family Papers)

Balances on Peons A/cs &c

Led.	Name	Amount	Note
8	Felix Chacon	25.65	Renter &c
10	Jesus Robles	1.45	"
14	Sostenes Salazar	87.74	Peon
20	Fermin Bernal	106.54	"
36	Procopio Escarciga	44.22	"
42	Juan de Dios Castillo	3.63	Renter
44	Eliseo Nijara	2.36	"
46	Mercedes Chavez	5.25	"
48	Toribio Salazar	11.27	"
52	Ignacio Cano	4.24	"
54	Dionisio Ramirez	8.53	"
56	Cruz Marquez	.90	"
58	Pedro Barriga	.21	"
60	Luciano Rubio	1.50	"
62	Dario Michondo	1.00	Zuloaga
64	Juan Murillo	9.07	Workman?
66	Sabino Cardenas	22.35	Renter
68	Refugio Estrada (Saenz	3.75	Saenz Administrador
70	Julian Robles	28.13	Renter
72	Hac.da Rubio (Zuloaga	42.53	Zuloaga
74	Manuel Chacon	6.61	Renter
80	Rafael Gomez	5.00	Zuloaga
84	Antonio Cisneros	4.24	"
86	Abram Cuevas	55.19	Peon
91	Librado Muñoz	1.69	Zuloaga
92	Francisco Saenz	5.00	Saenz covering mare
95	Reinaldo Ruiz	1.25	Rayada Saenz
		$487.10	

Sainapuchic Aug.t 11/901

General ledger balances for Oxsheer's Sainapuchic ranch in Mexico. (Oxsheer Family Papers)

F. G. and Mary (marked by X's) with a vacation group in Denver. (Oxsheer Family Papers)

The Oxsheer mansion in Fort Worth. (Oxsheer Family Papers)

F. G. Oxsheer's sons: *(top)* F. G., Jr., *(left)* Drennan, *(right)* Coke. (Oxsheer Family Papers)

The Diamond Ranch outfit. (Oxsheer Family Papers)

Left, a cowhand at the Diamond Ranch. *Right*, F. G. and Mary Oxsheer at Diamond Ranch headquarters. (Oxsheer Family Papers)

F. G. Oxsheer's "cotton patch" of five hundred acres near Stanton, Texas, pictured in the July, 1905, edition of *Texas and Pacific Quarterly* (Oxsheer Family Papers)

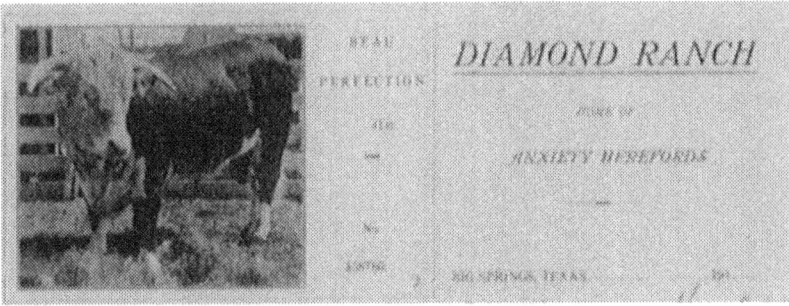

Letterhead of the Diamond Ranch business stationery. (Oxsheer Family Papers)

Dust storm near Stanton, Texas, 1931. (Oxsheer Family Papers)

F. G. Oxsheer, cattle king. (Oxsheer Family Papers)

CHAPTER II

Joys and Sorrows

When he returned to Texas, F. G. Oxsheer was a man. In his own way he had acquired the daring of a riverboat gambler. He wasted no money at poker tables or roulette wheels, but he was willing to spend his last dollar on longhorns, betting he could sell them for a profit. He bought and trailed a herd to Kansas every spring for the next several years, sometimes with the Beals, other times on his own, exchanging steers for gold and reinvesting in still more stock. By 1873 F. G. owned more than a thousand cattle. That same year his father was elected to the Texas legislature, marking the end of Reconstruction. The great ordeal was over; the Oxsheers had survived.[1]

That year was a turning point in many ways. For the first time in memory, F. G.'s thoughts were on more than longhorns, cattle trails, or even his mother and dad. There was a dark-eyed brunette he could not get out of his mind. She was Mary Beal, the sister of John and Nick. F. G. had known Mary all of her life. He had seen her for years at camp meetings, picnics, and horse races, but if he thought of her at all in the past, it was simply as the smiling girl with the freckled nose. Now Mary was a young woman with sparkling eyes and rosy cheeks. She was lively and happy, and she made F. G. feel the same way just by looking at him. John and Nick teased him about it. After all of the years and miles together on the cattle trails it seemed that all F. G. wanted to do was visit the Beals. They had no idea F. G. enjoyed their company so much, they told him. F. G. and Mary were married in May, 1873. She became his lifelong companion, the mother of his children, and the best friend he would ever have.[2]

---

[1] Edwyna Thro, interview with the author, Wichita Falls, Tex., May 30, 1983.
[2] Frances Hodges, "Memoirs," in possession of the W. A. Oxsheer family, Fort Worth, Tex.; Robert Beal, interview with the author, Fort Worth, Tex., June 30, 1983.

F. G.'s father gave them two hundred acres of Little River bottomland. The Beals added horses, mules, and a small herd of longhorn cattle—an appropriate gift. On their two hundred acres F. G. and Mary built their first home, a frame house with two rooms, a stone chimney, and a front porch—little more than a cabin. In front, a ragged entrance arch made of fence posts and wire welcomed visitors. Mary kept the yard swept clean as everyone did in those days, pulling up every sprig of grass and packing down the earth until it was like rock. In the back stood a smokehouse and a crude log barn. They furnished the little home with hand-me-downs from relatives and friends. In the main room were an old table with several chairs whose seats were made of cowhide, a quilt box, a spinning wheel, and a few other trifles. A cinnamon bearskin rug lay near the front door. The other room contained a walnut-frame bed, a chiffonier, and a trunk, but not much else.[3]

In March, 1875, Mary bore a child, Mabel, the first of eight. It was a happy time for the young parents; it was magic, looking into the eyes of that baby. The beaming father was certain she was the most beautiful in Texas and would no doubt marry a future governor. He made a special trip to Cameron to buy a crib. If some of his Chisholm Trail buddies had seen him riding along with a baby crib under his arm, they would have laughed themselves out of their saddles.[4]

All was not happiness and joy, however. The life of F. G. Oxsheer was in many ways the story of a father's love mixed with disappointment and crushing sorrow. A first son, Willie, named after the brother he had lost, fought two weeks for life, then died. In 1878 another son, Walter, was born. But like countless other children in the 1800s, the little boy died at the age of three, the victim of dysentery or "bloody flux." With a grief that only a parent could understand, F. G. paused to think of life and the great mystery beyond, of what his dead children might have become, and of the legacy he would someday leave when he too breathed his last.[5]

In 1880 a second daughter, Myrtle, was born, and two years later another son—F. G., Jr. There was something special between F. G., Jr.

---

[3] Edwyna Thro, interview; John Drennan Oxsheer to Frances Hodges, Nov. 24, 1957, and Oct. 24, 1964, Oxsheer Family Papers.

[4] Family Bible, Oxsheer Family Papers; Edwyna Thro, interview.

[5] Family Bible, Oxsheer Family Papers; John Drennan Oxsheer to Frances Hodges, Nov. 24, 1957, Oxsheer Family Papers.

and his father, a certain indescribable bond. Maybe it was the name, or the fact that F. G., Jr. was so bright and capable. In the years ahead there would be other children: another daughter, Mary, called by her middle name Beal; and two more boys, Drennan and Coke, the latter named for Richard Coke, the governor who ended Reconstruction. F. G. loved them all and spent his life smoothing their way, but somehow F. G., Jr. stood apart from the rest. He always seemed to embody his father's hopes and dreams.[6]

The Oxsheers were typical of their age. Mary ran the household according to the needs of her husband, serving breakfast at six, dinner at noon, and supper at six in the evening. If Fount was not yet home, everyone waited. The children knew they should be properly dressed and combed when they came to the table. Anyone who complained of the food or picked at the meal was promptly excused. "There's always a sufficient variety of food on my table for anyone to enjoy a good meal," their father would announce. "Evidently you're not hungry, so we'll excuse you now!" Before he had finished his words, the child would be leaving the room. He was a man who meant what he said, and his children knew it.[7]

At the same time he was tender and loving. On summer evenings the family sat on the front porch until bedtime. While Mary rocked or knitted in the dark, F. G. thrilled them with stories of the Chisholm Trail, stampedes and raging rivers, outlaws in Abilene, or sleeping wrapped in a blanket while curious animals walked up to sniff at him. Sometimes he sang—"Possum up a Gum Stump," "Watermelon Smilin' on the Vine"—keeping time, bouncing a giggling child on his knee. After the little ones were asleep F. G. and Mary sometimes sat up far into the night, discussing events of the day, planning for the future, or just listening quietly to the crickets and the mournful cry of the whippoor-will.[8]

After he married, F. G. quit the cattle trails to be with his family. While Mary kept the home, he earned a living as rancher and cattle dealer, buying and selling stock wherever he saw a profit. By now he

---

[6] Family Bible, Oxsheer Family Papers; Billy Oxsheer, interview with the author, Fort Worth, Tex., June 22, 1983.

[7] Hodges, "Memoirs."

[8] Hodges, "Memoirs"; W. A. Oxsheer, interview with the author, July 6 and 7, 1983, Fort Worth, Tex.; Edwyna Thro, interview.

was a shrewd cattleman; at a glance he could tell the age of a steer or correctly guess its weight within a few pounds. He also recognized that the cattle business was changing. In 1876 a man named John Gates had proved in San Antonio that a new invention—barbed wire—could hold the wildest longhorns. Barbed wire, F. G. realized, would close the cattle trails one day. Wire would also make it possible to keep one's cattle separate from others and to upgrade them by introducing Durham or Hereford bulls.[9]

Sometimes cattle dealing took F. G. from home for several days. Mary packed a brown alligator satchel, filled his flask with "ranch medicine," and kissed him good-bye. As much to keep her company at these times as to help with the chores, F. G. hired a family of orphans, two boys and two girls, children of former slaves. They remained with the Oxsheers for years. In time one of the boys became cook on F. G.'s favorite ranch; the other developed into a top cowhand. The girls, Kate and Noss, helped with the housework.[10]

No one knew it for years, but Noss was a kleptomaniac. Hardworking, dependable, honest in her own way, she was simply afflicted with an irrational and overpowering urge to steal. She often accompanied Mary when visiting neighboring farms and ranches, but after one visit a neighbor soon repaid the call to ask if the Oxsheers knew anything about the disappearance of her butter. Mary knew nothing about what might have happened, but the fact remained that each time she visited the woman, all of the butter vanished. Finally they called in Noss to see if she could solve the mystery. Noss freely confessed. She had taken butter from the neighbor's cookhouse and stored it on joists under the Oxsheers' house. She took them to the spot, and the two women knelt down to see for themselves—the wooden beams were oozing butter.

Once Mary and Noss received other more frightening visitors on a night when F. G. was away. They were in the main room with Mary's first baby, Mabel, when they heard voices in the dark, drawing closer to the house. Mary instantly remembered a rumor of escaped convicts. As the sound of voices grew closer she picked up the baby and ran with Noss into the other room. They hid behind the bedstead sitting at

---

[9] Billy Oxsheer, interview.
[10] Hodges, "Memoirs"; W. A. Oxsheer, interview.

an angle in the corner. The men came onto the porch, then clomped through the kitchen door without knocking. Looking for food, they rummaged about while Mary and Noss crouched behind the headboard in the other room. Gently Mary pressed the baby to her breast, hoping she wouldn't cry. After what seemed an eternity, the men found food and left, but the women remained behind the bed until they were sure it was safe. When they finally came out of their hiding place, all was quiet, save for the sound of crickets and the pounding of hearts.[11]

In 1882 the family moved to the town of Calvert in neighboring Robertson County, fifteen miles to the northeast. F. G. had considered moving since his days on the Chisholm Trail. In fact, the cattle drives and the Kansas railheads were what had given him the idea. By the 1870s the railroads in Texas had connected the Southwest with Northern and Eastern markets. This convinced F. G. that the trailing business would eventually become local. Texas drovers would trail cattle fifty or a hundred miles to the nearest railhead instead of five hundred or six hundred to the north. Equally important, stockyards and packing plants would arise just as they had sprung up in Kansas City after the opening of the Chisholm Trail. So why not get into the emerging meat-packing industry, he reasoned, before there was much competition? He didn't have the money to build a packing plant, but he could open a meat market at Calvert. If it did well, and if events developed as expected, in a few years he could construct a packing plant. It was a gamble involving most of what he owned, but if his hunch was correct, he would become a wealthy man. He could not have known then, but F. G. was correctly anticipating the development of the Texas cattle industry over the next fifty years.[12]

Calvert was one of those tough little boomtowns typical of the American frontier. It was at the head of a railroad connecting Central Texas with the Gulf Coast and Eastern markets, and also a starting place for those headed farther west. Throngs of sweaty men jostled in front of buildings, shouting prices for real estate or business ventures. Men, animals, and wagons clogged unpaved streets that were filled with choking dust in summer but turned to souplike mud in winter and

[11] Hodges, "Memoirs."
[12] John Drennan Oxsheer to Frances Hodges, Nov. 24, 1957, Oxsheer Family Papers.

spring. Hogs roamed everywhere, flies swarmed, and dead animals littered vacant lots, filling the air with their stench. Cursing teamsters and beefy dancehall girls; squint-eyed gunmen and fun-loving cowboys; gamblers and sharecroppers; ministers and merchants; railroad crews, drifters, and families heading west—all gathered in Calvert.[13]

Amid this rumpus the Oxsheers made a home. F. G. bought a frame house for the family, and on the edge of town he built his meat market, complete with sheds and feeder pens. At first he worked alone, but as business expanded, he hired others to help. Before long F. G. spent most of his time away from the market, buying cattle or contracting beef for eating establishments and boardinghouses. With the profits he bought several hundred acres in and around Calvert. He expanded his feedlots and entered the feeder-wholesale business as well, fattening and selling cattle to other butchers. Soon F. G. was one of the most prominent businessmen of Calvert, operating the largest meat market in town, slaughtering, dressing, and selling over the counter what he didn't sell on the hoof.[14]

Before long, drovers were trailing herds to Texas railheads, as F. G. had foreseen, and packing plants were springing up in towns like Denison and Hearne. The emerging Texas packing industry was small compared with those in Kansas and the Midwest, but it marked a beginning. Before long, Calvert, too, might have a packing plant. Nothing seemed to stand in the way, nothing except the town itself.

By the 1880s Calvert was a community with economic promise, a railhead in the heart of a developing cattle region. Local optimists were certain it would someday rival Kansas City as a beef market. But Calvert had a problem that stood in the way of these dreams. The town was virtually lawless, a wide-open place where shootings, thefts, and muggings were part of daily life. Thugs infested alleys, streetwalkers and confidence men hustled clients openly, and businessmen dared not return home on the same streets after dark. Law enforcement, such as it was, simply looked the other way, or spent its time hauling off the dead after a gunfight, and filling out useless reports. In Texas "civiliza-

---

[13] Richard Denny Parker, *Historical Recollections of Robertson County, Texas, with Biographical and Genealogical Notes*, pp. 27, 61.

[14] John Drennan Oxsheer to Frances Hodges, Nov. 24, 1957, Oxsheer Family Papers; Deed Records, vol. 9, pp. 249–50, vol. 13, pp. 19, 22–23, 26, 28, 31, Robertson County Courthouse, Franklin, Tex.

tion" was a recent thing; with some it was little more than skin deep. If one lived in a place like Calvert, it was with the knowledge that perhaps one in five was a thief or a killer. Without laws backed by firm enforcement, these types became utterly savage.[15]

One evening while the Oxsheers were at home, there was a knock at the door. Several merchants and community leaders had come to ask F. G. to run for sheriff, convinced he was the man for the job. They knew that in Abilene he had seen some of the deadliest gunmen in America—buffalo hunters, outlaws, and Civil War veterans who found it easier to keep on killing for hire than to work for a living. In one way he was like them; he could match guns with nearly anyone. Those who knew him swore that he was the finest shot they had ever seen. If Mary planned a chicken dinner, he simply stepped to the back porch with his Colt revolver and blew the head off a chicken—sometimes at a distance of thirty paces. But in a more important way, F. G. was nothing like these gunmen. He still retained the genteel habits of his plantation upbringing, a sense of duty and chivalry—the old code of honor. Proud and courteous, he was swift to act—sometimes too swift—but effective.[16]

F. G. explained he'd come to Calvert to earn a living, not tame a town. But the men wouldn't listen. They kept talking of the fate of Calvert, and of personal fears, even in their own homes. Several times strangers had entered private homes, claiming they mistook them for brothels. Killings had become so common, they said without smiling, that the town coroner "had a dead man for breakfast almost every morning."[17]

As F. G. listened to the strained voices and studied the anxious looks, he began to have second thoughts. He couldn't help but ask himself certain disturbing questions. What if a stranger entered his own home when Mary and the children were alone? And how would his father, William Oxsheer, have answered these men who were asking for the help only he could give? Twice his father had served in the Texas legislature at Austin; F. G. remembered how difficult it had been for

[15] John Drennan Oxsheer to Frances Hodges, Nov. 24, 1957.
[16] Billy Oxsheer, interview; Hodges, "Memoirs"; John Drennan Oxsheer to Frances Hodges, Nov. 24, 1957, Oxsheer Family Papers.
[17] John Drennan Oxsheer to Frances Hodges, Nov. 24, 1957, Oxsheer Family Papers; Parker, *Historical Recollections*, p. 83.

him to leave behind his home and loved ones. He also recalled why his father had gone: duty, public service, community responsibility. Like it or not, the old ways were still as much a part of F. G. as the cattle trails or life in Calvert. He finally agreed to serve as sheriff, but only for a single term. When the men asked what would happen then, they received a quiet but reassuring reply. By that time, F. G. told them, Calvert would be a peaceful town.[18]

F. G. Oxsheer was an imposing figure when he stepped onto the streets as the sheriff, a figure who commanded instant respect. There was something about those steely blue eyes—the way they looked into a man—his tall, ramrod frame, his air of confidence; he was almost magnetic. Other men the same size would have looked thin and willowy. Not him. He wore a dark suit, white shirt, and a Stetson hat creased with a Texas block. Strapped to his hip was a Colt "Peacemaker," oiled and spotless like his clothes. Only the handle looked worn from use. In a way he seemed transformed, but no one living could threaten his family. He brooked no insult, direct or implied. Men quickly learned that somewhere he had acquired a sense of honor that was best not impugned.[19]

From his own hard experience, F. G. had learned to handle guns like an expert. He had to, growing up in Milam County. During Reconstruction he had plowed wearing a pistol, keeping watch for renegades while he worked. The secret of a revolver, he knew, was to fire "within your range." He never shot a pistol except at a target twenty to thirty paces away, and he never practiced at any other distance. In time he developed an instinctive feel for his mark. He also knew that one bullet rarely killed instantly. Men who had been hit four or five times might keep firing; some had received fourteen wounds and lived. A gunfight, as much as anything, was a test of wills. The victor was usually the one who was determined above all else to empty his revolver into his enemy, no matter the cost.[20]

Even with a new sheriff the situation didn't improve at first. Cowed and timid jurors were afraid to convict lawbreakers, but when the

---

[18] Hodges, "Memoirs"; John Drennan Oxsheer to Frances Hodges, Nov. 24, 1957, Oxsheer Family Papers.
[19] Hodges, "Memoirs"; Billy Oxsheer, interview.
[20] Billy Oxsheer, interview; John Drennan Oxsheer to Frances Hodges, Nov. 24, 1957, Oxsheer Family Papers.

people saw that F. G. was determined to do his job, they finally rallied to his support. There was no courthouse in Calvert, but a merchant named John Drennan offered the second floor of his store as a courtroom. In Drennan the new sheriff gained both a friend and a trusted deputy. In the daytime F. G. and John patrolled the streets in shifts; in the evenings they made their rounds together. A good deputy was worth his weight in bullets in a place like Calvert.[21]

Rowdy cowboys in town for drunken sprees were more noise than danger, F. G. knew from past experience. They responded to fairness and tact, but they would fight any man, including a sheriff, if they believed they had been mistreated. If several rode their horses into a store or shot up the mirrors and ceiling of a hotel lobby, F. G. became simply an arbiter between owners and fun-loving drunks. Cowboys generally paid their fines and damages and held no grudge.

Another element, however, was not so easily handled. A number of saloons and brothels were under the influence of a type of organized crime. Cardsharps, confidence men, and prostitutes fleeced the patrons of these places. If a person was too wily to be conned, he was robbed at gunpoint; if he fought back, gunmen hired as guards or bouncers would kill him. Another ploy involved prostitutes and the killing of clients by gunmen posing as avenging husbands or lovers, the old "badger game." After a shooting, the girls and the killers divided the victim's money. Behind swinging doors drifted the sounds of poorly played pianos, shrill laughter, the click of poker chips, and nearly every night, the angry pop of gunfire.[22]

There was no "Code of the West" among these gunmen. The people who made their living this way were murderers who shot unarmed victims in the back or from behind walls or out of dark alleys. They wore a pistol on the hip, and usually kept a second tucked out of sight in a shoulder holster or a boot.

The trick to handling these types was a quick, overwhelming show of force—doubled-barreled shotguns with hammers cocked and fingers on triggers. In saloons or on the streets this was the safest, surest way to confront troublemakers. Sawed-off shotguns in the hands of determined peace officers probably did more for law enforcement in frontier

---

[21] Hodges, "Memoirs."
[22] John Drennan Oxsheer to Frances Hodges, Nov. 24, 1957, Oxsheer Family Papers.

towns than all the six-guns ever made. Soon F. G. and John Drennan were familiar figures stepping into saloons with shotguns in hand—the sheriff through the front door, his deputy through the back. Whether making nightly rounds or dealing with trouble, they carried their formidable weapons. Two shotguns fired in unison could pacify a room full of the most deadly gunmen.

In an amazingly short time Calvert began to resemble a well-policed community. F. G. seemed to be everywhere, riding through the streets, walking down once dangerous alleys, or in and out of saloons. A few of the killers and cardsharps challenged him at first, but they quickly learned that the soft-spoken sheriff with the courtly manners was someone to be taken seriously. Underneath the dignity, the poise, and the genteel bearing was a resolute and dangerous man. The swift blaze of fury in those blue eyes, the lowered lids, the tightened jaw—to confront him with a gun, in the words of one who knew him, meant a shotgun blast or a bullet in the head.[23]

The county jail was the largest building in Calvert, a two-story structure resembling a fortress. It was generally filled with cowboys or local rowdies sleeping off hangovers or spending a day or two behind bars for disturbing the peace. But occasionally the "guests" were hardened criminals or killers sentenced to years of hard labor and awaiting transfer to the state penitentiary in Huntsville. It was F. G.'s duty to haul them to prison.[24]

It was a lonely ride from Calvert to the East Texas town of Huntsville. For several days F. G. drove the prison wagon over winding roads through dark, towering forests. All day he drove the team of mules, with no one for company but the shackled men in the wagon bed behind him. Before dark he left the road and made camp, sometimes by a stream, but usually in a dreary pine barren. He kindled a fire and cooked supper, then released the men to eat one at a time. Afterward he settled back against a log or a tree, pistol strapped to his hip, shotgun across his lap. The prisoners lay on the ground, chained to wagon wheels and to one another at the ankles. It would have been easy for F. G. to drift off to sleep after a long day, but he didn't dare. He could

---

[23] John Drennan Oxsheer to Frances Hodges, Nov. 24, 1957, Oxsheer Family Papers; Edwyna Thro, interview.

[24] John Drennan Oxsheer to Frances Hodges, Nov. 24, 1957, Oxsheer Family Papers.

only stare into the crackling fire and doze off for a few minutes at a time until dawn. He never lost a prisoner on the road to Huntsville.[25]

True to his word, within a year of taking office F. G. had made Calvert a law-abiding town. Before long, accounts of crime and violence were mostly stories that parents told their children. Years later, when all of Central Texas was settled and frontier times in Calvert were but a memory, many would attribute the rise of law and order to the coming of the railroads, to Prohibition, or to the building of churches and schools. But old-timers would always recall a lean young man named Oxsheer who tamed a wide-open town with a shotgun, a long-barreled Colt .45, and iron nerve.[26]

Calvert settled down, but it was destined never to rival Kansas City. In fact, it hardly grew at all through the remainder of the 1880s. The railroad continued on farther west, and the town was no longer the end of the line. Soon the county government also moved to the rival community of Franklin. Business declined, property values fell, and families moved away. Calvert was no place for a packing plant.[27]

The Oxsheers were one of the first families to leave. F. G. could deal with hoodlums and gunmen, but fighting a slumping economy was hopeless. He sold his meat market, land, and cattle for forty thousand dollars, packed the family in a wagon, and moved farther west to the town of Lampasas. Disappointed though he was about his plans for a packing plant, he was already looking ahead for other opportunities. Their new home was in a pretty little town nestled amid limestone hills covered with cedars and post oaks. The community had seen its share of violence and bloodletting in the past because of Reconstruction and the Horrell-Higgins feud, but Texas Rangers had brought law and order in 1877. It was said that Lampasas had one of the best school systems in the state, and Mabel was old enough to start. Lampasas seemed like a good place to settle as a cattle dealer or rancher, or even to open another meat market.[28]

[25] John Drennan Oxsheer to Frances Hodges, Nov. 24, 1957, Oxsheer Family Papers.

[26] John Drennan Oxsheer to Frances Hodges, Nov. 24, 1957, Oxsheer Family Papers.

[27] A packing plant opened near Calvert in the 1880s, but failed for lack of operating capital as well as the loss of railhead status—the same problems that confounded F. G. Oxsheer. Parker, *Historical Recollections*, p. 83.

[28] John Drennan Oxsheer to Frances Hodges, Nov. 24, 1957, Oxsheer Family Papers.

By now the cattle industry was riding a crest of prosperity, the so-called beef bonanza. A combination of technology and rising incomes was responsible. Refrigerated railroad cars and steamships had linked Western cowmen with hungry wage earners on the East Coast and in European cities. The great stream of Texas cattle pouring north along the Chisholm Trail had signaled the beginning of this era. Soon, men lured by the promise of huge profits were establishing ranches and cattle herds in every part of the central and northern plains. As buffalo and Indians were driven from the prairies, cattle replaced them in ever-increasing numbers, forming a vast pastoral empire stretching from South Texas to the Canadian border.

Individuals as well as cattle companies established ranches. They built crude headquarters shacks along streams and filed claims for the land running up and down each bank. In this way cattlemen could graze stock on either side free of interference, for once they controlled both sides of a stream, they were masters of the water. Equally important, they ruled by default all of the surrounding watershed without actually owning the land. As long as open range and free grass remained, a cowman could make a fortune.

Among those determined to establish a ranching empire were Mary's brothers, Nick and John. The two had been in West Texas since the 1870s, still driving cattle to Kansas and running their own freighting business as well. Now they were in Colorado City, heart of the West Texas cattle country, forming the Jumbo Cattle Company, and inviting their brother-in-law, F. G. Oxsheer, to join them as a partner.[29]

It didn't take F. G. long to decide. He knew that other cattlemen in the area were amassing fortunes: Tom and Dudley Snyder, C. C. Slaughter, Charles Goodnight, and many more. On a summer morning in 1884, with two mule-drawn wagons, the Oxsheers pulled out of Lampasas, headed for Colorado City. F. G. had bought into the Jumbo Cattle Company.[30]

Maybe it was only natural that he was moving west, settling on the frontier. For more than 150 years the Oxsheers had lived on the cutting edge of the English-speaking world. They came with the early settlers to Virginia's Shenandoah Valley and were among the first to cross the mountains into eastern Tennessee. When F. G.'s father, William Ox-

---

[29] Hodges, "Memoirs"; *A Guide to the South Plains of Texas*, n.p.
[30] Hodges, "Memoirs."

sheer, settled in Milam County, he was virtually alone for several years. Now, like his ancestors, F. G. was riding west to build a new life.[31]

He rode on horseback beside the wagons. Mary sat on the riding board of the lead wagon, holding two-year-old F. G., Jr. One of the servants handled the team. Mabel and Myrtle rode inside, occasionally poking their heads out to see. The second wagon carried the other servants and most of the family furniture.[32]

There were no bridges over streams or rivers, but nearly every streambed was dry or little more than knee-deep. Only the Colorado River was a problem. At the Colorado F. G. unhitched the mule teams and drove them across to the other bank. Next, the servant boys ferried over the contents of the wagons on crude log barges. Mabel and Myrtle crossed the river on their father's horse, one in front of him and holding the saddle horn, the other hanging on from behind. Then came F. G., Jr. His father carried him carefully, child in one hand, reins in the other. Finally, the two boys pulled the floating wagons to the other bank one at a time with ropes, while F. G. rode as close to them as possible. If the wagon began to tip over, those inside had orders to jump for his horse. The wagons swayed like ships at sea, but there were no mishaps, and in a few hours everyone was safely across.[33]

Soon a familiar routine developed. They traveled an average of twelve to fifteen miles a day—about the same as herds on the cattle trails. Every morning they rose before sunup, usually to a cloudless sky and a steady southwest wind. By dawn they were on the road, a rutted limestone trail. The sun rose, the wind died, and the locusts began their incessant screeching, announcing another day of heat. All day they creaked along, heading northwest until late afternoon when again they camped.

At first they often camped by farmhouses where families usually offered them a meal or even a bed. But as they moved west, signs of habitation grew more scarce. Before long it was a matter of bedding down miles from anyone—children in the wagons, adults on the ground. There were certain dangers that came with sleeping on the ground; campers were occasionally attacked by rabid skunks or stung

[31] Hodges, "Memoirs"; William Oxsheer to F. G. Oxsheer, June 2, 1900, Oxsheer Family Papers; Deed Records, Book C, Roll 34, pp. 176–79, State of Tennessee Archives, Nashville, Tenn.
[32] Hodges, "Memoirs."
[33] Hodges, "Memoirs."

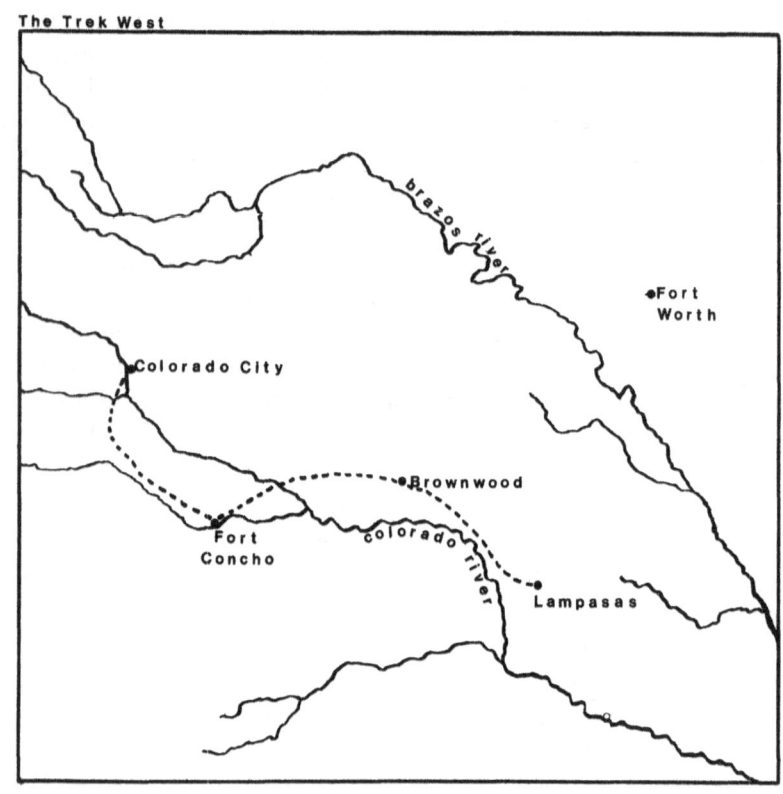
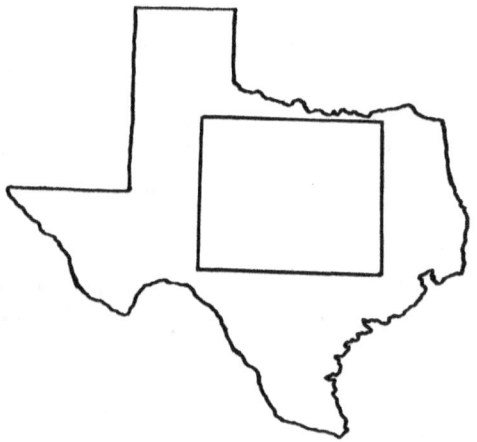

by scorpions and centipedes. Everyone had heard of the man who was stung to death by a centipede. While building a fence, he put his jug of drinking water in the shade of a bush, where a centipede fell from a limb and dropped inside. When the man took a drink, he swallowed the insect, and it lodged headfirst in his throat. Struggling to pull it out, he tore it in half.[34]

Fortunately the Oxsheers had no troubles with night creatures. They traveled for more than two hundred miles through the Colorado River valley to Brownwood, then west to Fort Concho before turning north to Colorado City. For the first few days the country was familiar limestone hills covered in brush and chaparral, draws filled with cedars, oaks, and occasional massive pecan trees. But slowly the land and vegetation changed. Trees grew gnarled and stunted, oaks two centuries old rose no higher than a man's head. Pitifully warped for lack of moisture, they clung to the soil, struggling to survive in a hostile environment, until finally, a little farther west, they could not survive at all. The hills gave way to a vast, grass-covered plain that stretched away toward a bluish horizon. Only the distant mesas and the stems of countless yucca plants broke the monotony of the plains. There were no mesquite trees, no fences or telegraph poles, scarcely anything but sky and grass.[35]

Ahead of them heat waves shimmered and danced, occasionally changing into a mirage resembling a cool lake. To the left or right whirlwinds or dust devils spun their slender columns upward, picking up dirt and trash as they crossed spots bare of vegetation. Occasionally a herd of wild mustangs circled them, taunting the mules, sometimes coming within fifty yards of the wagons. At times a roadrunner appeared in front of the wagons, leading them for a distance, trotting along at the same speed. Overhead, buzzards circled against the backdrop of blue, gradually becoming smaller and smaller until they disappeared.

They traveled on for weeks, until at last they were within a day of their new home. Behind F. G. lay his boyhood, Reconstruction, the cattle trails, and Calvert. Ahead was a new life on the West Texas plains, the pursuit of a new dream, the building of a ranching empire. One more night on the ground, one more day in the wagons—next stop Colorado City.

[34] Hodges, "Memoirs."
[35] J. W. Williams, *Old Texas Trails*, ed. Kenneth F. Neighbors, n.p.

CHAPTER III

The Awesome Plains

"Next stop Colorado City!" The startled old man lurched forward in his seat, blinked, then looked around at the half-empty coach car and at the conductor walking down the aisle. F. G. had been dreaming—the cattle trails, his marriage, the births of his children—all were dreams of an old man about the past, memories somehow brought to life again in his sleep. The conductor plodded on to the other end of the car, announcing Colorado City, gently touching the shoulders of napping passengers as he moved along. Bleary-eyed, F. G. looked out the window into the dark. The train was slowing down, and in the distance he could see lights. In a few minutes they would reach the station.

F. G. stared out the window, wondering how the old place must look. He had been in and out of Colorado City for more than half his life, but had not set foot in town for several years. For some time now Colorado City had meant only a string of lights on the Texas plains—a half-deserted whistlestop he passed through on the night train to Fort Worth.

Colorado City had once been a center of the range cattle industry, headquarters and home for more cattlemen, perhaps, than any other town on the western plains. Following the roundups cowhands poured into the community by the hundreds, some from as far away as New Mexico. Men crowded hotel lobbies, restaurants, and bars, or gathered on street corners to deal in cattle. In a boomtown atmosphere the sound of hammers banging on unfinished buildings filled the air, while riders came and went, and men spoke of range conditions or speculated about the price of beef. Even after fifty years F. G. remembered clearly the crowded streets, the ornate hotels, and the cattle pens near the edge of town. Settling back into his seat, he also recalled the first time he had ridden into Colorado City, mounted on a buckskin stallion, followed by family and servants in wagons. It seemed like yesterday, that hot afternoon in July, 1884, when he first rode into the town.[1]

---

[1] The date of F. G. Oxsheer's arrival in West Texas is uncertain. One of Oxsheer's

Cattle cars were the first things they saw, hundreds of them lining sidetracks for more than a mile, marking the edge of Colorado City. There were also great heaps of buffalo bones awaiting shipment east to be ground into fertilizer. Not until F. G. led the family wagons to the other side of the railroad cars and bone piles could they see the town.

Afternoon shadows filled the streets as the family made their way into Colorado City. They had been on the road for weeks, moving like gypsies from one campsite to the next. Now at last, they had reached their new home. Weary, dust covered, they moved along, no one uttering a sound—no one except F. G., Jr. Kicking and screaming, he wanted down from the wagon so he could ride on his father's saddle.[2]

They rode through the middle of town to a house F. G. had rented, silently looking forward to a night in a bed under a roof. But as they plodded along, nearly at the end of their journey, F. G. was troubled. Everywhere he looked were gambling dens and dancehalls, cowboys staggering about the streets, some arm in arm with painted women. It was Calvert all over again. As they rode farther, however, the scene changed—Colorado City was more than saloons and dancehalls. They passed restaurants, stores, theaters, and even an opera house. One of the restaurants—Jake's—was said to have the best food in West Texas. Even in Calvert F. G. had heard of Jake's. Next came stone and brick buildings, two and three stories high, with the names of nationally renowned cattle firms on signs across their fronts; then churches, ostentatious mansions, and even a park with a zoo. Rowdies were restricted to a certain area. The town was in the hands of Dick Ware, one of the most effective lawmen in Texas. Determined, fearless, and a dead shot, Sheriff Ware had a way of bringing out the peace-loving side of human nature.

It was dusk when they pulled up in front of their new home. Everyone unloaded whatever he or she could carry: children handled blankets and lamps, adults struggled with bedsteads, mattresses, or trunks. In the twilight they made their way onto the front porch and

---

children wrote that he settled in Colorado City in the summer of 1882, while another stated it was July, 1884. Deed records on this matter are also contradictory. If he arrived in 1882, Oxsheer's significance as a pioneer cattleman is even more noteworthy (see chapter 4). To underestimate rather than exaggerate his place in history, I used 1884 as the time of arrival in West Texas. John Drennan Oxsheer to Frances Hodges, Nov. 24, 1957, Oxsheer Family Papers, Fort Worth, Tex.; Frances Hodges, "Memoirs," in possession of the W. A. Oxsheer family, Fort Worth, Tex.

[2] Edwyna Thro, interview with the author, Wichita Falls, Tex., May 30, 1983.

entered the house. A few minutes later Kate and Noss were preparing beds. But as they worked in the lamplight, one of them noticed something crawling on the floor—the house was alive with bedbugs. Instantly, Mary Oxsheer ordered the unloading stopped. Everything was taken outside, and once more the family slept under the stars. The following morning everyone went to work clearing the house of pests. Cans filled with water went under bedposts, while turkey feathers dipped in coal oil were used to douse every nook and cranny.[3]

For several days they washed and scrubbed; not until Mary was convinced the house was free of crawling things did they move in. But once the family was comfortably settled, F. G. turned his thoughts to what had brought him to Colorado City—the Jumbo Cattle Company. In a few days he packed his saddlebags, kissed Mary and the children, and swung into the saddle; Jumbo headquarters was forty miles to the northwest. It was hard to say good-bye, knowing he would not see his family again for months. It seemed that he was forever away from those he loved most. But Mary assured him everything would be all right and urged him not to worry. As F. G. loped away on horseback, he could barely hold back his excitement. Over the horizon a whole new life was about to unfold.

The Jumbo range was enormous, more than half a million acres spanning four counties, stretching fifty miles along the Double Mountain Fork of the Brazos River. It was the stuff of dreams and empires—a rolling grassland threaded by arroyos and clear-running streams. There were other cattle firms or even individuals with more land—a few controlled more than a million acres—but none possessed a finer range.[4]

Rising from Jumbo's southern border was Muchakooaga Peak and two or three nameless mesas. Resembling enormous pyramids of a lost civilization, they stood in endless vigil, changing colors in the afternoon sun from blue-green to yellow-orange, and finally sunset gold. Forming the western boundary of the Jumbo range was part of a three-hundred-mile-long escarpment called the Cap Rock, an abrupt geologic dividing line. Above the Cap Rock to the west stretched the Llano Estacado or Staked Plains, endless miles of uninhabited flat-

[3] Hodges, "Memoirs."
[4] Robert Beal, interview with the author, Fort Worth, Tex., June 30, 1983; Hodges, "Memoirs."

lands. To the east were the Low Plains, the Double Mountain Fork, and the Jumbo range. Wedged along the base of the Cap Rock were cedar brakes, thickets of wild plums and grapes, even an occasional oak or cottonwood tree. Watered by shallow ponds and intermittent springs, the trees eked out an existence. For ages the springs and ponds had served as gathering places for man and beast. Around their banks lay remains of abandoned campsites, tracks of antelopes and deer, and the fossilized bones of creatures long extinct. In the past the springs and ponds had refreshed Comanche raiders, white trappers, and countless numbers of buffalo. Now they watered the Jumbo cattle—twenty-five thousand Texas longhorns. Hidden in the cliffs of the Cap Rock were the lairs of wolves and mountain lions; higher up, perched on crags, were the nests of eagles.[5]

In many ways the Jumbo Cattle Company was a tremendous gamble. It represented most of the combined savings of F. G. Oxsheer, John and Nick Beal, and two other men who remained in Central Texas: J. T. Davis and F. G.'s old friend and deputy sheriff, John Drennan. But the Jumbo was more than money, land, or even cattle; it was above all else people—the men who rode the range. Chief among them was John Beal, the general manager and largest stockholder. The veteran cattleman had faced his share of challenges on cattle drives to Kansas and in West Texas: Indian attacks, cattle rustlers, stampedes, inclement weather. Still riding step for step with John in every encounter was Nick, another who knew the cattle business and the harder side of life.[6]

There were also cowboys who worked for forty dollars a month and a home called Jumbo. Several had come from neighboring outfits like the Long S Ranch of C. C. Slaughter. A few were farm boys who had come west looking for adventure. Experienced cowhands called them "lints." It was said that lint still clung to their clothes after so many years of dragging cotton sacks. Others were relatives, such as Richard Beal, a brother of Nick and John. At age sixteen he had joined Hood's Texas Brigade, one of the most renowned fighting units in the

---

[5] John Drennan Oxsheer to Frances Hodges, Nov. 24, 1957, Oxsheer Family Papers; Mrs. Frank Miller, interview with the author, Gail, Tex., Oct. 11, 1983.

[6] Articles of Incorporation of the Jumbo Cattle Company, Oct. 29, 1883, Oxsheer Family Papers; John Drennan Oxsheer to Frances Hodges, Nov. 24, 1957 and Oct. 24, 1964, Oxsheer Family Papers; Robert Beal, interview; W. A. Oxsheer, interview with the author, Fort Worth, Tex., July 6 and 7, 1983.

Confederate army. In the fighting at Gettysburg, Richard was wounded four times before he fell and was taken prisoner. Near the end of the war he was paroled from a New York prison camp and walked home to Texas, where he found work in a lumberyard. Now Richard was on the Jumbo branding and herding cattle.

Another brother who worked for a time with the Jumbo Cattle Company was "Gulf" Beal, a gruff, no-nonsense individual who later made a name for himself with his own land and cattle. For as long as they lived, Gulf and Nick were teased for ending the political career of their close friend Sheriff Dick Ware. The two of them rode from the Jumbo to Colorado City on election day for the sole purpose of voting for Ware. Leaving before dawn, they stopped in early afternoon to rest their horses. Along a shaded ravine the two men unsaddled their mounts and stretched out for a short nap. But when they awoke it was dark, the election was over, and Dick Ware had lost by a single vote.[7]

Finally, there was another brother, A. A. "Turk" Beal. There were stories about Turk's younger days in Central Texas, rumors about fence cutting and ransacking towns. When drunk, it was said, he used to ride into town and begin tearing apart some of the stores, slashing feed sacks with his Bowie knife or throwing saddles through windows, and no one dared interfere. In a day or two his father would show up, pay for the damages, and all was forgotten—at least until the next time.

No one but the family was certain about the truth of these rumors; no one else would have dared to ask. Turk was a huge, barrel-chested brute with massive shoulders and twice the strength of most men. Once, a bobcat leaped from a ledge onto a horse Turk was riding, landing on the saddle horn, literally in the rider's lap. The horse pitched off man and beast, but not before Turk seized the bobcat by the legs. Once on the ground he killed the animal with his bare hands, slinging the dazed cat through the air and snapping its spine with the power of his grip. Turk was not a man to anger.[8]

They were rugged people, the men of the Jumbo, and about the only amusement they enjoyed on the range was pulling pranks. If a

---

[7] Hiley Boyd, Jr., interview with the author, Lubbock, Tex., June 13, 1983; John Drennan Oxsheer to Frances Hodges, Nov. 24, 1957, Oxsheer Family Papers; W. A. Oxsheer, interview; Edna Clark Miller, "Jumbo Ranch," *Borden Citizen* 4, no. 4 (June, 1969): 2; Robert Beal, interview.

[8] W. A. Oxsheer, interview.

tenderfoot was in camp, he was warned of rattlesnakes before he stretched out for the night. If he chose to sleep in the chuckwagon, cowhands told him of the horrible "pohelia monster." Far more poisonous than a rattler, they cautioned, it had a peculiar affinity for wagons and could slither up a wheel as quickly as a lizard runs up a tree. One common trick began before everyone turned in for the night. Experienced cowhands steered the conversation to the many poisonous, slithering creatures that inhabited the plains: rattlesnakes, scorpions, centipedes. The next morning the cook yelled breakfast and everyone put on hats and boots, but as one of the new hands slipped on a boot something inside seemed to reach up and wrap itself around his toes. With a yell he jerked off the boot and threw it as far as he could while everyone else roared with laughter. A big hunk of sourdough would be sticking to the victim's foot, squashed between the toes.[9]

At ranch headquarters the new hand was given the sleepy-looking outlaw horse, regaled with horrid tales of venomous tarantulas, hydrophobic cows, and quicksands that could swallow up horse and rider in the twinkling of an eye. If the tenderfoot took it all in stride, showed himself a good sport, and laughed along with everyone else, he was eventually admitted into the charmed circle of the Jumbo outfit. But woe unto the luckless individual who failed to take the hazing as good fun; he was driven from the country, written off as a Yankee or a sheepman.[10]

What a bunch—pranksters and war veterans, grizzled cattlemen and green farm boys, a town-tamer who looked and behaved for all the world like a tidewater planter, and a bobcat-killing wild man. They were a strange mix, but no one bothered them. A troublemaker might have ended up saddled and ridden around a corral like a bronc, shot dead, or grasped by the powerful hands of someone threatening to snap his spine.

In some ways their lives were similar to those of the Indians they replaced. The longhorn was their buffalo. The spectacle and socializing event was not the hunt but the roundup, a time when widely separated men came together. The cattlemen lived off different beasts and held different totems—not the antelope or bear, but the Circle Dot, the

---

[9] W. A. Oxsheer, interview; Hodges, "Memoirs."
[10] Hiley Boyd, Jr., interview.

Buckle B, and the Flying L—the sacred brands. Like the Indians, too, the ranchers never truly understood the industrial world that ultimately destroyed their open-range way of life. Their horizons were endless, their wants few. They lived off the land and loved it perhaps as much as any Comanche.

There was no spacious ranch house to mark the Jumbo headquarters, no bunkhouse, no stables or barns—nothing but a few corrals and a two-room frame dwelling. The days of palatial ranch homes were still far away. Even on the largest ranches West Texas range life in the 1880s was primitive. F. G. spent his first summer with the Jumbo Cattle Company at a lonely camp in the shadow of the Cap Rock, with nothing for shelter but a covered wagon bed. "They just set the wagon bed off on the ground and left me there," he recalled later, leaving him with no one for company but his horses and his thoughts.[11]

Sometimes in the evenings, when the moon was full and wolves howled from the top of the Cap Rock, F. G. must have wondered whether he was truly alone. A few years before Comanches had raided near the spot where he camped, taking dozens of horses belonging to the Beals; several men had been killed. It was the last Indian raid in Texas, but F. G. had no way of knowing that at the time.[12]

Probably he also remembered old family stories of life in Milam County when red man and white struggled in a ceaseless, guerrilla war for possession of the land. Once his mother and father nearly lost their lives in an Indian raid. They were visiting relatives: women sat across the cool front porch rocking, dipping snuff, and gossiping, while children scampered up and down the steps. Out in the yard men squatted under enormous cottonwoods, laughing and joking; farther away slaves were grinding corn. Suddenly there was a stir, a gunshot, and Indians burst from the woods, sending everyone racing for the cabin. Women and children dashed into one room and slammed and bolted the door. Men and slaves leaped onto the porch, then rushed into another room across an open hallway from the women. But one slave failed to reach the cabin. Indians swarmed about him, beating and slashing. Inside William Oxsheer and the others looked for a way to help, but how? Guns were across the hall behind locked doors with the women. There

[11] Hiley Boyd, Jr., interview; Miller, "Jumbo Ranch," p. 1.
[12] Mrs. Frank Miller, interview; *A Guide to the South Plains of Texas*, n.p.

was nothing to do but listen to the shrieking, piteous cries for help from a man writhing in agony.[13]

As the campfire died away, F. G. leaned against his wagon bed, listening and wondering what lurked in the dark. The sound of the wind, loose pebbles falling from the Cap Rock . . . was someone out there? What of that bush near the cliff, had it moved in the last hour? Was it even there the night before?

Every morning F. G. rose at dawn, stirred the hot coals, put on coffee, then cooked a breakfast of bacon and sourdough biscuits. After eating, he saddled a horse then rode off to begin the day. His job was "riding line," following an unmarked boundary separating the Jumbo range from neighboring lands to the southwest. When he happened upon cattle with the Buckle, ⊖, or Buckle B, ⊖B, brand of the Jumbo Cattle Company, F. G. headed them toward the home range. If the cattle were from another ranch, he shooed them back in the direction they had come. It was an all-day chore, and generally uneventful. Sometimes he rode for hours, seeing nothing but jackrabbits, antelope, or an occasional set of buffalo bones. Other times he happened upon a cow and her calf, two or three steers, or occasionally a few dozen head.[14]

At noon F. G. stepped down from his mount and took a biscuit and a slice of beef from his saddlebag. He often wondered how Mary and the children were getting along in Colorado City as he sat eating in the shade of his horse. After eating he sometimes hobbled his horse and stretched out on the ground for a nap, using his saddle as a pillow and his Stetson to keep off the sun. As long as a man could find shelter from the sun, he was usually comfortable. The arid West Texas winds had a way of easing the heat. Rested, he saddled up and rode back the way he had come, returning to camp an hour before dark. In one way riding line was like trailing cattle—the greatest problem was generally boredom.[15]

By the end of summer, F. G. had given up his wagon bed for new quarters, a dugout cut into a bank five or six feet deep, covered with a roof of poles and dirt. It was primitive but practical in a land without timber and also reasonably warm in winter and surprisingly cool in

---

[13] Hodges, "Memoirs."
[14] Hiley Boyd, Jr., interview; Miller, "Jumbo Ranch," p. 1.
[15] Hiley Boyd, Jr., interview.

summer. The dugout was scarcely noticeable from ground level. Only a small chimney and a buffalo robe hanging from a passageway gave a clue that it existed.

Inside was a table, chairs, a washtub, a pot-bellied stove, and for cooking, a coffeepot and skillet. Anyone visiting his dugout would have found it typical of others, with one exception: on the stove was a flatiron fashioned from a brick. When time allowed, F. G. worked on his clothes. He was determined to have pressed shirts and even continued wearing his old suits. He must have been the most fastidious cowboy on the West Texas plains.[16]

All went well for F. G. and his partners. Beef prices mounted steadily through the fall of 1884. The Jumbo steers sold for a remarkably high price, and the weather remained pleasant. On the plains, men said, the future was as boundless as the horizons. But they would soon have reason to change their minds.

For several days in early January, 1885, the weather was unseasonably warm; temperatures were in the seventies and balmy winds blew in from the Gulf. Then it hit. First a streak appeared on the northwest horizon, looking like another Cap Rock but darker in color, ominous, and moving rapidly closer. Suddenly the wind changed from the same direction, an icy blast that no amount of clothing could protect against. A cold rain began to fall, quickly changing to sleet. Within minutes the temperature had plunged forty degrees; a few hours later it was near zero. Sleet changed to heavy snow, a blinding, streaking white, driven by winds that rose to forty, then sixty miles per hour. Winter had arrived on the West Texas plains.[17]

All day it raged, the winds and the snow never letting up. Occasionally F. G. pushed back the buffalo robe from his dugout, then stepped outside, squinting out into the blizzard, searching for what he knew must come his way. At dusk, in the worst part of the storm, he caught a glimpse of them for the first time—the cattle. Driven by the

---

[16] The description of the dugout is taken from the one on exhibit at the Texas Tech University Ranching Heritage Center. This dugout, though generally attributed to Col. C. C. Slaughter, was first inhabited by F. G. Oxsheer. For several years the dwelling served as headquarters for one of Oxsheer's ranches. Hiley Boyd, Jr., interview; Hodges, "Memoirs."

[17] Don H. Biggers, "From Cattle Range to Cotton Patch," *Frontier Times* 21, no. 4 (Jan., 1944): 163–65; David J. Murrah, *C. C. Slaughter: Rancher, Banker, Baptist*, p. 57.

violent wind they drifted before it, strung out single file in a half dozen lines. When blizzards struck, they would drift south until the winds stopped or they dropped dead from exhaustion. Nothing could force them back into the storm. Cattle would stumble single file into a river, crashing through the ice, drowning by the hundreds, only to be followed by hundreds more walking over the bridge of carcasses to the other bank.

F. G. stepped back inside, slipped on his thickest coat, and picked up his saddle. There was nothing to do but follow the cattle until the winds stopped and they could be headed back. The number of cattle in the drift was impossible to estimate. Most of them belonged to the Jumbo, but the blizzard swept along every cow or steer in its path. A few of the lead steers were already passing near the dugout, their backs covered with ice, their hoofs crunching in the snow. F. G. knew it would be a long night. He pushed past the buffalo robe and went out to his horse, hoping the storm would soon let up. It was more than a simple matter of being cold; the survival of the Jumbo herd was at stake.[18]

All through the night the blizzard raged. By dawn the snow had stopped, but the merciless winds still howled. F. G. thought of cooking breakfast, then catching up with the herd, but the winds prevented kindling a fire. There was nothing to do but ride on, from time to time nibbling on frozen biscuits or jerky packed in saddlebags. At daybreak, he saw that drifting columns of cattle had begun to concentrate into a single enormous herd strung out for miles. For the first time he was aware that other men were also following the cattle. In the distance were cowhands from the Jumbo and from neighboring ranches to the south. It hadn't occurred to him that he was on his neighbor's range, that the Double Mountain Fork was miles away. For the remainder of the day F. G. and the others followed the herd, watching the cattle drift south. Not until dark did the wind finally calm and the herd stop, more than twenty-four hours after the blizzard had begun.

The following morning every cloud had disappeared; a perfect calm settled on the plains, while sunshine glistened on a vast expanse of white. The cattle, exhausted by their long march, lay on the ground where they had stopped the night before, strung out as far as the eye

---

[18] Edwyna Thro, interview.

could see to the north. Some were too weak to rise again. No one could guess how many more had already been lost in rivers and frozen bogs. Slowly the men began to push the weary herd north.

It took a week to gather the Jumbo cattle and drive them homeward. Yet no sooner had the cattle begun to drink through the broken ice of the Double Mountain Fork than another blizzard struck, more furious than the first. Men looked at one another in amazement, wondering what was happening. They had seen cold before, but nothing like this. What they did not realize was that climate on the plains is cyclic. Since white men had arrived in West Texas, the summers had been moist, the winters mild. Settlers had poured into the West, slaughtering buffalo and stocking the plains with herds of Texas longhorns—more cattle than the land or the changing climate would ultimately support. Now stock by the tens of thousands would perish, and many ranchers throughout West Texas would lose everything. A third blizzard hit, and then a fourth, but no one bothered to ride after the drifting herds again. Men fell to their knees and prayed that their cattle would survive until spring. Somewhere the ghosts of old Comanche warriors smiled, their view of the land and nature vindicated at last.[19]

By spring scarcely any cattle remained within a hundred miles of the Jumbo range. The survivors had drifted south to the lower Pecos and Devil's rivers; a few had even made their way to the Rio Grande and the Mexican border. There was only one way to retrieve the cattle. Range outfits from throughout West Texas would have to work together in a massive roundup. From the Jumbo came every available hand—F. G., John and Nick, Gulf and Turk—to take part in the greatest roundup in West Texas history.

Almost everything about the roundup was on a grand scale. On the first day the outfits gathered more than eight thousand head from the canyons and cedar brakes of the Pecos. Protected from cold winds in the Pecos River Canyon, more cattle had survived than anyone had believed possible. But because of the sheer numbers of men and cattle involved, it was impossible to hold the herd until the last animal was reclaimed. While some men continued separating longhorns from the brush, others began to drive cattle north every few days. One of those selected to drive the first eight thousand was F. G. Oxsheer. Only men

---

[19] Edwyna Thro, interview; Hodges, "Memoirs."

with trailing experience were entrusted with the task, for no one before had ever driven so many cattle successfully. The drive from the Pecos was something F. G. never forgot. It turned into one of the most harrowing experiences of his life.[20]

They would travel slowly northeast for a hundred miles to a spring called Bull Run, then another forty miles to the Concho River before fanning out to individual ranches. Bull Run promised only limited water; men and horses might get enough to drink, but the cattle would have to suffer. Until they reached the Concho, 140 miles away, the herd would have no water. It was a desperate plan. Many cattle already weakened by the winter would die of thirst, but there was no other way to salvage the herd. By pushing the cattle every hour, day and night, it would take more than one hundred hours to reach the Concho and water—more than one hundred hours in the saddle.

As the men drove the cattle north, order and system broke down. It was one thing to handle two or three thousand head on the Chisholm Trail, another to drive eight thousand across more than a hundred miles of waterless landscape. As soon as the longhorns started north they began to string out in familiar fashion, the strongest steers taking the lead, the weaker ones following. Before many hours the herd had stretched out for miles in an unmanageable column. When the men left the Pecos they took three wagonloads of water, enough they thought, to carry riders and mounts to Bull Run. But long before they had reached the spring, there was scarcely enough water left to wet parched lips.

The weather was hot for spring, already in the nineties, the ground still barren from winter. Soon the effects of heat and parched earth began to show. The cattle bawled piteously for water—a half-choked bellowing. Occasionally the lead steers happened upon bushes or stunted trees. Smelling the moist green leaves, they dashed ahead, obliterating the spot in a swirling mass of water-crazed longhorns. If they reached bushes, not a vestige of the plants would be left; if trees, nothing remained but a few twisted splinters. Every twig and particle of foliage was stripped and eaten within minutes.

For three days and nights they pushed north without stopping. At first, men grew irritable for want of sleep, but as hours slipped into

---

[20] Edwyna Thro, interview.

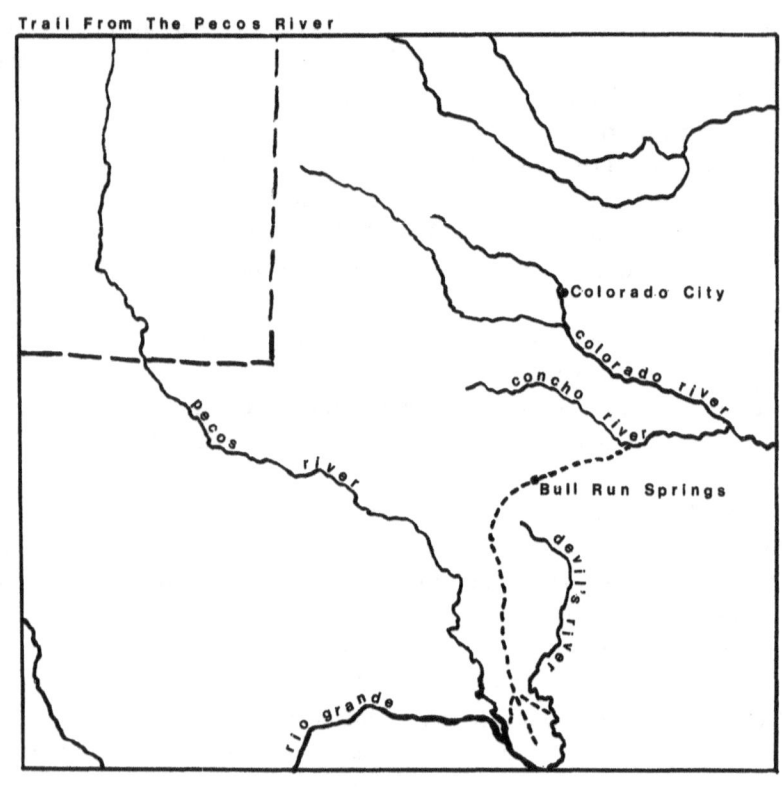
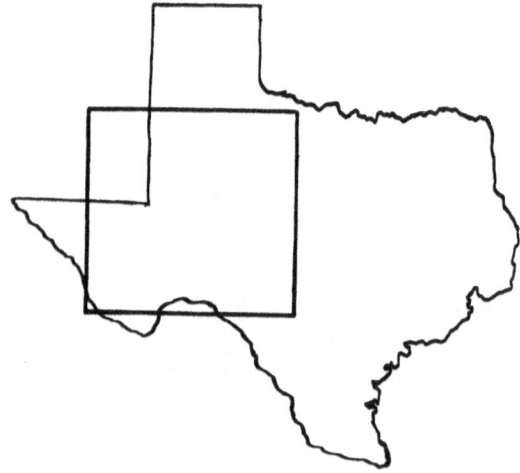

days, they grew dull and listless. Some slept in the saddle, occasionally falling from their horses, hitting the ground with a thud. A few pulled off the trail and stretched out for an hour or two, but most simply went without sleep. No one worried about stampedes; no one had the energy to care. By the end of the second day, their only concern aside from sleep was whether any of the herd would survive. The trail was already littered with dead and dying longhorns.

Miles before they reached Bull Run the lead steers raised their heads, sniffed the air, then picked up the pace. The herd smelled water. Soon those with enough strength broke into a trot, then finally a run, racing ahead of the men on horseback. Exhausted, throats parched, the riders followed, thinking of nothing but the refreshing spring ahead. But when they finally reached it, what they found was sickening.

Throughout the winter cattle had huddled in the surrounding ravines where they had frozen to death by the thousands. For more than a mile, wherever there was a trace of water, the ground was covered with rotting, stinking carcasses, and over them thousands of cattle scrambling to sip mud and filth. A few of the men pulled up their bandanas to filter the odor, then tried to find a drinking place for the horses. Other drovers, nearly frantic with thirst, began to dig a hole nearby, hoping to catch a bit of seep water for themselves. They formed a circle around the hole to fight off the maddened cattle until at last they filled a few buckets with the "muddy, foul stuff."[21]

There was no time to rest. The herd was nearly mad with thirst and the Concho River was still forty miles away. F. G. and the other men climbed back into their saddles, drove the cattle from the mud, and headed north again. Those last miles the animals no longer walked, they shambled along, eyes sunken, heads lowered. When they smelled water for a second time, near the Concho they didn't rush ahead, they staggered. Of the eight thousand that set out from the Pecos, less than half remained.

At the end of the nightmare men collapsed in exhaustion; some slept for a day and night without rising. Men, cattle, and horses lingered near the Concho for several days more, still half-stunned by what had happened. But within a week cowboys began to separate by brands what was left of the herd, then fanned out to the surrounding ranches with the cattle. The Jumbo range was still a hundred miles

---

[21] Edwyna Thro, interview.

away, but at least the country ahead was graced by an occasional stream. For the next two months F. G. traveled back and forth from the Concho to the Double Mountain Fork, picking up Buckle B cattle that others brought north from the Pecos. It had been a hard winter, followed by a terrible spring, but in some ways, troubles had only begun.[22]

The history of West Texas is the story of a people struggling with the awesome force of nature. More than Indians, isolation, or material privation, the relentlessly changing climate was the greatest challenge: blizzards, hailstorms, tornadoes, and above all, searing heat and drought. When rain fell the land resembled an enormous park. But when the skies were cloudless for months or even years at a time, temperatures soared and the grasses withered and died. Wildlife left the land, hung on by a thread, or fed the circling vultures. The once beautiful park became a battleground for survival between nature and all living things.

The spring of 1885, following the unprecedented winter, saw the beginning of one of the worst droughts in West Texas history. For fifteen months it failed to rain. The earth cracked and turned hard as the native limestone. Streams dried up, while springs once thought of as unfailing simply vanished. Cattle that had survived the winter now died by the hundreds, their bones bleaching in the sun. A few cattlemen had water shipped by rail to Colorado City and hauled it by wagon to their ranches. But even this trickle for the cattle was eventually cut off; as wells began to fail in Colorado City, all water was diverted for human use. Every cloud in the burnished sky offered hope, until after months without rain, there was no hope. One could flee the path of a flood, take shelter from a blizzard, but from a drought there was no escape.[23]

The drought was a wrenching experience for the Oxsheers and the Jumbo Cattle Company. While Mary stood in line in Colorado City for her daily water ration, F. G. watched his cattle die of thirst, the same cattle he had exhausted himself to retrieve from the Pecos River. By the end of summer, men on the Jumbo were skinning hides from carcasses, selling them for three dollars apiece. Within a year they counted only a few thousand gaunt, pitiful forms still scavenging the burned-out range—less than half the original herd.

[22] Edwyna Thro, interview.
[23] Mrs. Frank Miller, interview.

By a freak of nature not uncommon on the plains, rangelands to the north of Texas had escaped the blizzards and drought; in Kansas, Wyoming, and the Dakotas cattle still grew fat and men kept building herds. But in the winter of 1886–87, their day of reckoning also came. Massive blizzards killed more than half of the North Plains stock. In the spring the same drought that had gripped West Texas spread northward, not only through the rest of the plains but also into the corn belt of the Midwest, the region that purchased feeder cattle. Throughout the plains, cattlemen suddenly faced the ultimate peril—the loss of a market. From Texas to Canada they rushed to sell what remained of their cattle to packing plants in Chicago and Kansas City. Just as quickly, prices collapsed as a result. Cattle that brought high prices a year before could hardly be sold.

Winters without parallel, endless droughts, and finally a market without bottom—the beef bonanza was finished. Virtually every large operator was broke or teetering on the brink. Conrad Kohrs of Montana, the Dolores Cattle Company of Texas, the Dickey Brothers, and the Swan Cattle Company of Wyoming, to name but a few: all were ruined or close to it. Many smaller ranchers were wiped out to the last animal. The awesome plains, it seemed, would overwhelm the foolish men who had dared think of it as home. For some, perhaps for most, it was too much. They spat on the cracked ground, cursed the cloudless skies, and left without looking back.

Still, not everyone departed. Some remained because they had no place to go, but others hung on, determined to build anew. These men, the cattlemen who remained to rebuild their herds, were a tough, resilient people, at their best in a crisis. They knew how to deal with adversity, how to bend without snapping, and how to fight back. Among them was F. G. Oxsheer. Leaning against a corral fence at the Jumbo headquarters, he scanned the western horizon, but not for rain. He was staring at the Cap Rock, thinking about the land beyond the great cliffs—the Llano Estacado. The lean Texan had a plan.

CHAPTER IV

A Cattleman's Legacy

THE first time F. G. Oxsheer heard of the Llano Estacado, he was fascinated. It was a last frontier, one of the largest unclaimed grasslands remaining in America. A handful of cattlemen grazed stock along the eastern fringe and on the Canadian River in the Texas Panhandle. Two hundred miles to the west others raised cattle and sheep in New Mexico's Pecos River Valley. Between the Texans and the ranchers of New Mexico, however, in an area as large as the state of Indiana there were probably fewer than a dozen settlers. It was a land of antelope, wild mustangs, and endless vistas.

In its own peculiar way the Llano Estacado, the Staked Plains, was extraordinary country. Stretching beyond the rugged Cap Rock, the surface formed some of the most perfectly level terrain on earth. Covered only with grass and yucca plants, the region seemed to reduce all creation to land and sky. The few who ventured into the region were always in danger of losing their way, for every mile traveled seemed identical to the last. Even the vegetation conspired to confuse; as one rode along on horseback, the trampled grass soon straightened up, erasing all evidence of a path. There was a special quality about the Llano Estacado, something men had tried to put into words since the days of the Spanish conquistadores. The endless plains, the "sea of grass"—when men spoke of the land, it was in hushed tones of respect and awe.

The Llano Estacado had defied settlement by whites for centuries. Lacking surface water except for lakes and ponds that often dried up, serving as a favorite hunting ground of the peerless Comanches, it was a place frontiersmen avoided. The Spanish had explored and claimed the land as early as the 1540s, but when they finally relinquished title in 1821, not one of them inhabited the Staked Plains. Mexico claimed the land next, followed by the Republic of Texas and

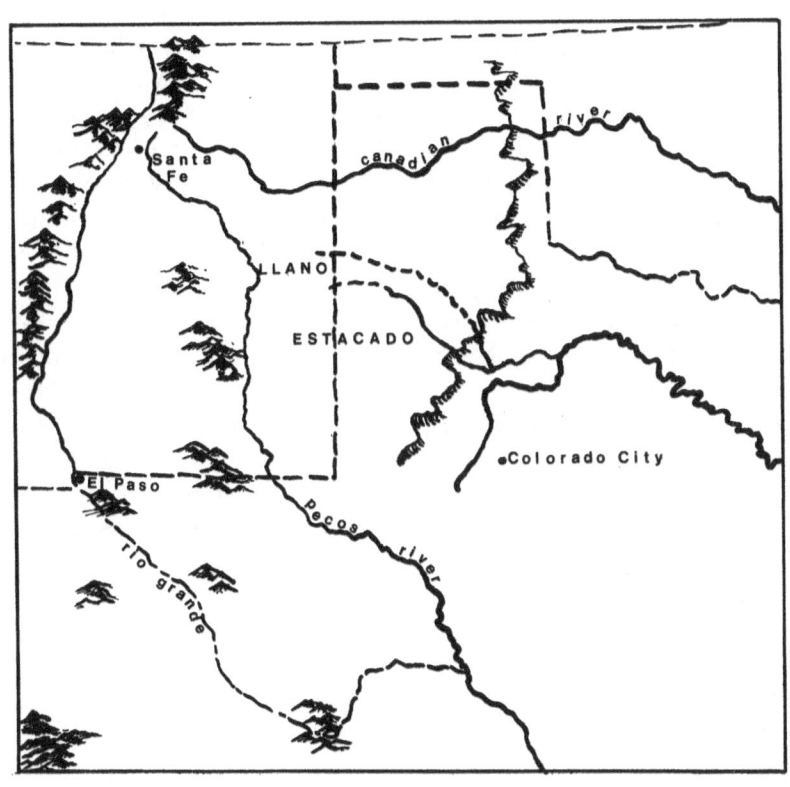
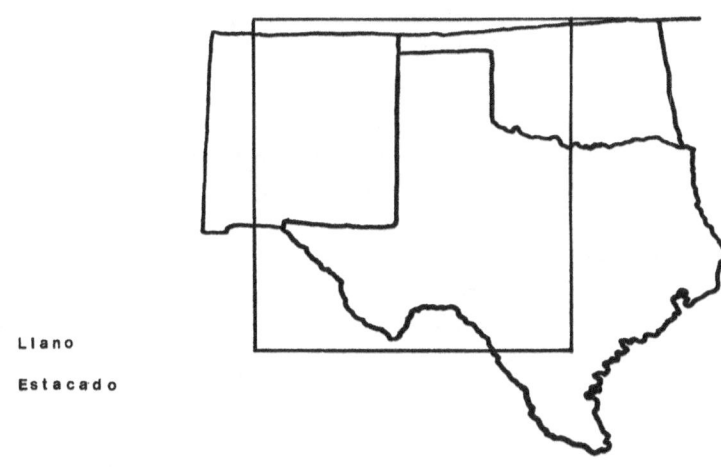

Llano Estacado

the United States, yet the country remained wild and free. *Ciboleros* and *comancheros*, New Mexico buffalo hunters and traders, had crossed the region, but none had settled there. By the time F. G. Oxsheer arrived in West Texas, both Comanches and buffalo were gone, but the land was as open and wild as the first time Coronado's men gazed upon its vastness. Over the southern half of the area there was nothing to give the slightest hint of impending settlement, nothing but a solitary figure riding along the rim of the Cap Rock in the summer of 1884.[1]

Soon after he became part of the Jumbo Cattle Company, F. G. Oxsheer rode out onto the Staked Plains. He had heard about this land that resembled an ocean; half curious, half skeptical, F. G. wondered what to expect. What he found was unforgettable. The Staked Plains contained the finest rangeland he had ever seen—it was a cowman's empire waiting to be seized. True, there was no surface water for cattle and horses in many places, but that no longer mattered thanks to the introduction of well drilling and windmills. Cattlemen were already drilling wells and putting windmills on land a few miles to the east, bringing water to the surface where there was none before. With wells and windmills, a man could transform the plains into a rancher's paradise. The land, owned by the state or set aside for support of public schools, cost only fifty cents or a dollar an acre, and leased for pennies, and even these prices were misleading; if someone chose to graze stock without paying for the land, who would be around to object? Who would even care? All that was needed to establish a ranch was a herd and a few windmills. As he rode across the flatlands, F. G. figured the cost of a ranch: well drillers, cattle, horses, corrals, hired help. He had invested most of his money in the Jumbo Cattle Company, but he still had enough at least to start another ranch.[2]

He was not the only one impressed by the possibilities. Just to the north the giant XIT Ranch was contracting for cattle and advertising for hands to work the three-million-acre spread. In the state legislature politicians who had never seen the land laughed and joked about the XIT and the "fools" who planned to graze cattle on West Texas sand, but F. G. Oxsheer was not laughing once he had seen the country. He realized that cattlemen would soon pour into the region, clamoring for

---

[1] Frances Hodges, "Memoirs," in possession of W. A. Oxsheer family, Fort Worth, Tex.

[2] Hodges, "Memoirs."

land. By the time he had ridden back to Jumbo headquarters, F. G. was determined that when the others arrived he would already be firmly established there with a ranch of his own. Before the end of 1884 he was grazing stock in the heart of the southen Llano Estacado, seventy miles west of the Cap Rock.[3]

He never thought of himself as a figure in history, but F. G. Oxsheer was one of the first to establish lasting settlement on the Staked Plains. Some had tried to ranch the country, but only a few had gained a foothold. The dugouts constructed for himself and his hands, the corrals of cedar posts and caliche rocks, were little more than specks on the landscape, but they were harbingers of things to come. Sitting on the open plains, the lonely ranch was in the van of settlement, pointing the way for thousands. By the summer of 1885 F. G. had wells drilled and windmills erected, perhaps the first on the Staked Plains. Before the 1890s he had also marked off much of the countryside with roads that would serve in the following century as county, state, and federal highways. "Build them straight," he told his men, "and keep out of the sand." There were a number of pioneer ranchers leading the western migration: the Goodnights and the Slaughters, the Littlefields, the Iliffs, and dozens more like them. Their effect on frontier America was immense, but on the Llano Estacado no one was more significant than the soft-spoken, enterprising cattleman with the unlikely name, Fount Oxsheer.[4]

When the great blizzards of 1885–86 decimated herds throughout West Texas, F. G.'s cattle suffered along with the rest. Drifting before the bitter winds, many plunged over the Cap Rock like a "living Niagara." But when drought and the collapse of beef prices followed,

[3] The site of this ranch is in present-day Hockley and Cochran counties. F. G. called it the Diamond Ranch and later renamed part of it the Ancient Briton Ranch. I have avoided using the Diamond name here to prevent confusing it with another Diamond Ranch he established later. See chapters 7 and 8 for a description of this second Diamond Ranch. Hodges, "Memoirs"; Hiley Boyd, Jr., interview with the author, Lubbock, Tex., June 13, 1983; Lillian Brasher, *Hockley County, 1921–1971: The First Fifty Years*, p. 21; Hiley Boyd, Jr., to David Murrah, June 2, 1970, interview, Oral History File, Southwest Collection, Texas Tech University, Lubbock, Tex.; *A Guide to the South Plains of Texas*, n.p.

[4] Hodges, "Memoirs"; Hiley Boyd, Jr., interview; Brasher, *Hockley County*, p. 21; Hiley Boyd, Jr. to David Murrah, Southwest Collection, Hiley Boyd, Jr., to David B. Gracy, Jr., May 19, 1969, Interview, Oral History File, Southwest Collection; *A Guide to the South Texas Plains*, n.p.

threatening to ruin every cattleman on the plains, F. G. was in a unique position. If it failed to rain in West Texas for a year or two, and if prices remained low for the same period, it mattered little. His cattle could eat parched grass down to the roots, then move to the surrounding range, for as late as 1887 he was still virtually alone. East of the Cap Rock, where the range was crowded and grass failed, thousands of cattle died from thirst and hunger, but on the Llano Estacado his stock thrived. Wherever his windmills turned in the breeze, his cattle flourished, and until the great drought broke and prices rose, F. G. was prepared to put in wells and windmills all the way to New Mexico if necessary.[5]

Drilling wells, building windmills, and driving hungry cattle from one range to another, F. G. held on under the worst conditions. In the meantime, he made plans for the future, plans that ultimately established him as one of the greatest cattlemen of the Southwest. He didn't see the 1887 collapse in cattle prices as the end; more than anything, to him, it simply marked the close of one ranching era and the beginning of another.

F. G. knew that the time to invest in cattle was while prices were low and that every dollar he could borrow should be used to buy as many head as possible. Everywhere he looked and everything he saw or read convinced him this was the right thing to do. Those who gave up and left were people who had never understood that the cattle market, like the weather, was subject to periodic change. Boom times were almost always followed by a collapse, then a bottoming out, and finally a rise in prices and renewed prosperity. In the following century economists would label this phenomenon "the business cycle," but for F. G. Oxsheer in 1887 it was simply a matter of experience and horse sense. He had seen it before in 1873; prices collapsed only to climb again to record levels. He was certain it would happen again. Steers that earlier had sold for $150 currently brought only a few dollars, if they could be sold at all. But if past experiences meant anything, a rise in prices would surely follow, and in a few years the same cattle would be worth more than ever. With a few thousand dollars a man could buy a herd that would someday be worth a fortune. Best of all, the Llano Estacado provided a nearly endless supply of grass to carry the stock until better times returned.[6]

[5] Edna Clark Miller, "Jumbo Ranch," *Borden Citizen* 4, no. 4 (June, 1969): 2.
[6] Hodges, "Memoirs."

F. G. had no cash; he had spent it all on windmills, land, and cattle, but he still had family and friends willing to entrust him with their money. His mother and father, still living in Central Texas, remembered how things had been following the Civil War, when F. G. had rebuilt their lives; they would lend money to their son. So would John Drennan, F. G.'s old friend and former deputy. In more ways than one the loan from his friend was something F. G. never forgot—he named his newborn son John Drennan Oxsheer. Others were also willing to make loans: A. J. Harris and M. B. Huling, two West Texas cattlemen; his in-laws the Beals; several state banks; and even a European investment firm.[7]

Gradually F. G. acquired a sprawling range stretching from the Cap Rock nearly to New Mexico. Spreading out from his original holdings, he began grazing cattle to the immediate southwest in an area later called the Mallet Ranch. Before long his growing herds ranged across a quarter of a million acres. Farther southeast he established the Tahoka Lake Ranch, 140,000 acres; and with John and Nick Beal he acquired another quarter million acres near the New Mexico border. He owned several brands on these ranches: the 99, the F, and the Old Jumbo Buckle, ⊖. But at last F. G. settled on the Lazy Diamond, ◇. More than just a brand, the Lazy Diamond practically became a coat of arms. F. G. was often away from his ranches, tending to his investment in the Jumbo Cattle Company, but more and more his thoughts and future centered on the Staked Plains. Soon the drought broke, and the demand for feeder cattle revived. Beef prices rose, and on the Llano Estacado there was a cattle baron named Oxsheer with thousands of longhorns to sell.[8]

Selling his stock in a market where prices steadily improved, F. G.

---

[7] Personal note, F. G. Oxsheer to William Oxsheer, July 19, 1887, Oxsheer Family Papers, Fort Worth, Tex.; Hodges, "Memoirs"; Vendor's lien, F. G. Oxsheer to A. J. Harris, Colorado City, Tex., Aug. 1, 1887, Oxsheer Family Papers; Bank note, F. G. Oxsheer to the Farmers and Mechanics National Bank, Fort Worth, Tex., Aug. 24, 1890, Oxsheer Family Papers; Vendor's lien, F. G. Oxsheer to the American Freehold-Land Mortgage Company of London, Limited, Dallas, Tex., Sept., 19, 1889, Oxsheer Family Papers.

[8] The site of the Mallet Range is in present-day Hockley and Cochran counties. The Tahoka Lake Ranch was in Lynn County while the Beal-Oxsheer Ranch was in present-day Cochran County. Hodges, "Memoirs"; Hiley Boyd, Jr., interview; Deed Records, vol. 2, p. 194, Lynn County Courthouse, Tahoka, Tex.; Deed Records, vol. 1, p. 4, Cochran County Courthouse, Morton, Tex.; Deed Records, vol. 1, pp. 174–80, Hockley County Courthouse, Levelland, Tex.; Hiley Boyd, Jr., to David Murrah, Southwest Collection.

prospered. There were setbacks of course. A blizzard in March, 1890, killed thousands of West Texas cattle; a drought in 1892 was followed by a money panic the next year. There was personal sorrow, too. In 1893 F. G.'s mother Martha Oxsheer died; she had been sickly since Reconstruction. F. G. grieved like any son, but death was not so shocking or unbelievable in those times; it was accepted as part of a natural order. He kept on working and continued to expand. In the late 1880s and early 1890s he purchased or leased a series of ranches east of the Cap Rock on the Rolling or Low Plains: the Doc Grounds Ranch in Taylor County, the Fen Ranch east of Sweetwater in Nolan County, and a horse ranch in Haskell and Stonewall counties. Next he acquired even more land on the Llano Estacado, buying the Surratt Ranch of 33,000 acres, and in the late 1890s, leasing the 93,000-acre Huling Ranch. No one in the Southwest controlled a more intricate ranching empire.[9]

Supervising this scattered network of ranches was not easy. A man could work hard, make wise decisions, and still lose everything. He was at the mercy of the elements as well as the market, and had no control over either. Droughts or blizzards might devastate his herds. When steers were ready for marketing, a sharp decline in beef prices might mean selling them at a loss. The cowmen who kept on ranching despite disasters no longer did so because they expected to become wealthy, but because it was the only way of life they cared to live. Only a few built ranching empires and made fortunes like F. G. Oxsheer's.

For a time F. G. held the horse ranch with several men, including W. T. Waggoner. Other pioneers of the range, W. T. Waggoner and his father Dan, had carved an empire of their own along both sides of the Red River in North Texas and Indian Territory. In the late 1880s Waggoner and F. G. Oxsheer were breeding thoroughbreds and quarter horses to mustang mares. In time they might have established their ranch as a leader in breeding mustang crosses, but the partnership later dissolved in a disagreement over use of the land.[10]

Dozens of cowboys worked the Oxsheer ranches, and probably a

[9] The Surratt and Huling Ranches were in present-day Cochran County. Hodges, "Memoirs"; Hiley Boyd, Jr., interview; Deed Records, vol. 2, pp. 304, 309, Taylor County Courthouse, Abilene, Tex.; Deed Records, vol. 2, pp. 27–30, Hockley County; Deed Records, vol. M7, p. 350, vol. M8, p. 486, vol. 1, p. 259, vol. 9, p. 532, vol. 15, p. 388, vol. 17, p. 87, Haskell County Courthouse, Haskell, Tex.; Deed Record, vol. 1, pp. 239–40, Cochran County.

[10] Hodges, "Memoirs"; Deed Record, vol. 15, p. 388, Haskell County.

few were a little leery of the boss at first. He was a fair man, and a polite one, but he wasn't like any cattleman they had ever known. He didn't smoke, chew, or dip; wouldn't get drunk; didn't even cuss; and his work clothes—dress suits—what a notion! Occasionally one or two drifters signed on, thinking they had found an easy way to pick up a dollar. What could a dude in a suit know about cattle or which men did their work? These types didn't last.[11]

On the Oxsheer ranches everyone worked from sun to sun and during roundups, far into the night. Anyone who didn't like the rules was free to quit. The ones who stayed on and did their work received as good a wage as any cowboy in Texas. Those who wouldn't carry their load were paid their time and given half a day to be off the land. The boss knew exactly what his men were doing; since he was nineteen, he had spent his life at the same kind of work.[12]

He also had a way of knowing if anyone was rustling his cattle. For years F. G. kept a mental account of his stock—cows, bulls, calves, horses, mules—thousands of animals on more than half a dozen ranches. He could go onto any of his ranches and recognize on sight hundreds of his cattle; it was uncanny. Any animals sold or found dead were deducted from the list; newborn calves were added. If his actual tallies fell short of the mental figures at roundups, the missing cattle were assumed stolen and the authorities notified. It wasn't easy to steal cattle from F. G. Oxsheer.[13]

Perhaps the finest all-around hand F. G. ever had was a man named Hiley Boyd. A tall, rangy fellow from the cotton fields of Central Texas, Hiley came west to be a cowboy when he was twenty-one. Maybe F. G. saw a little of himself in the young man, remembering how excited he'd been when he had first gone up the trail. Whatever the reason, he hired him when they first met in Colorado City. "Just sit in the saddle and let your feet dangle," F. G. told him, "then follow me." Most cowboys would work day and night in the saddle, through heat, rain, or snow without complaint, but were insulted if asked to do any chore on foot. Hiley Boyd was not one of these. He could ride and rope with the

[11] Edwyna Thro, interview with the author, Fort Worth, Tex., June 30, 1983; Hodges, "Memoirs."

[12] Edwyna Thro, interview; Hodges, "Memoirs."

[13] Billy Oxsheer, interview with the author, Fort Worth, Tex., June 22, 1983; W. A. Oxsheer, interview with the author, July 6 and 7, 1983, Fort Worth, Tex.

best of them, but he also greased windmills, hauled supplies in wagons, built dugouts, worked as a cook or a cowboy, or did any job that was necesasry.[14]

Fortunately Hiley was even-tempered as well as hard-working, otherwise F. G.'s dry, straight-faced humor might have been irritating. "Go easy in serving the red beans," F. G. often told him. "Red beans don't come cheap, you know." Beef, sourdough biscuits, dried fruit, or even luxuries like canned goods the men could have in abundance, but "go easy" with the beans, probably the cheapest food in Texas. Once, before leaving the Surratt Ranch for a couple of weeks, F. G. took the young hand aside and solemnly handed him a list of chores to complete before he returned. The list included drilling wells and repairing windmills, branding calves, and building roads—work that would take two or three years. Hiley simply nodded in agreement, swung into the saddle, and rode off with his list. When F. G. returned, he was delighted with the "good start" Hiley had made.[15]

Like most Texas ranchers F. G. generally had several black cowhands working for him. Some of the large outfits along the Gulf Coast hired almost no one but blacks. Former slaves or the children of slaves, many of them had handled cattle and horses for as long as they could remember. Some were bronc busters whose skills were legendary.[16]

Perhaps the most talented cowboy working for F. G. Oxsheer was a black man named Slick. No one knew Slick's last name; it was rumored he had killed a man in Louisiana. None of the others pried into these matters, however; in the West a man's past was his own affair. What mattered was the way Slick handled horseflesh. Every morning he was at one of the ranches busting the wildest broncs. While other cowboys perched on top of corral fences watching, Slick went to work.[17]

Inside a corral of wooden rails were several broncs, backs humped in the early morning chill. They were small in comparison with Eastern horses, but spirited, strong, and incredibly quick. Slick would climb over the fence and into the corral. Usually a boy in his teens was

[14] Hiley Boyd, Jr., interview; John Anna Dean Boyd, "Hiley and Margaret Boyd," undated manuscript, Southwest Collection, Texas Tech University, Lubbock, Tex.

[15] Hiley Boyd, Jr., interview; "Hiley and Margaret Boyd," undated manuscript, Southwest Collection.

[16] Hiley Boyd, Jr., interview; Hodges, "Memoirs."

[17] Hiley Boyd, Jr., interview.

with him. After Slick roped a bronc, the youngster would grab it by the ears, clamp the end of one ear between his teeth, then cover the bronc's eyes with his forearms. Slick saddled the animal and eased onto its back, pulled his Stetson down tight, then nodded to the boy—turn it loose.

Squealing and pitching, the bronc leaped, changing ends in midair, and crashing to the ground with a neck-popping thud. It was savage yet beautiful, man and horse struggling for mastery, the act of riding a wild beast transformed into an art. Sometimes a horse reared and with a vicious squeal, toppled backward, pinning to the ground anyone but an expert rider. For Slick, it was all in a morning's work. If a bronc pitched, he simply hung on, leaning forward and backward, pulling on the hackamore rope. If the horse fell backward, he nimbly dismounted before the animal could fall on him. Still clutching the hackamore, Slick placed his foot on the saddle horn when the kicking horse rolled over on its side, held the animal down for a moment, then as it struggled to its feet, slipped back into the saddle.

Sometimes a horse barely pitched at all. Instead, it raced across the corral and smashed into the fence, stunning horse and rider. At other times an animal would begin circling the fence perimeter, trying to rub off the man on its back. It was not easy busting broncs. Men were sometimes crippled for life by the sudden jolts and falls. A rider could be thrown and kicked in the head, or a saddle turned under a horse's belly while his foot still hung in the stirrup. For Slick, however, and for only a handful of others, the work was routine.[18]

Bronc busting in the morning sun and handling cattle on the open range—it was a way of life old-time ranchers and cowboys, black or white, never forgot, but it could not last. Ranching on the Llano Estacado has passed through only two stages in its hundred-year history: the open-range era ushered in by pioneers like F. G. Oxsheer, and controlled stock raising. Technological inventions, particularly barbed wire, signaled the coming of the new age. In the 1890s the plains were crisscrossed with wire fences. Longhorns vanished like the buffalo, replaced by white-faced Herefords and other selected breeding stock from the East and Midwest. Open-range roundups came to an end, and

---

[18] Hiley Boyd, Jr., interview.

old-time cowboys went the way of the Comanches. One by one, pistol-toting cowhands who had survived blizzards, droughts, cattle rustlers, and other calamities were replaced by fence menders, posthole diggers, and young men from agricultural colleges whose tools were the latest scientific information. Many of the ranchers would not survive the change, for it was too much to comprehend and not at all to their liking. But others, like F. G. Oxsheer, accepted what was inevitable, gave up the old ways and embraced the new, just as they had overcome the end of the Cotton Kingdom and the antebellum South thirty years before.

Stringing barbed wire across the landscape was nothing new to F. G. As a young man in Central Texas he had been one of the first to fence his land. He was also accustomed to dealing in blooded stock as well as longhorns, for in those days he had owned a few head of Hereford cattle. As early as 1893 he began to fence some of his West Texas ranches and stock them with white-faced Herefords, but this was only the beginning. He continued the practice until his ranches and his cattle were famous throughout the land.[19]

In 1895 legendary Texas cowman Charles Goodnight retired, selling his herd of purebred Herefords to a ranching neighbor of F. G. Oxsheer. More than just a herd of cattle, the Goodnight stock was some of the finest on the North American continent. As soon as F. G. saw the herd, he tried to buy it, but was unable to meet the price. Convinced the future of the cattle business lay in controlled breeding and upgrading and aware that such a herd would make him a leader in the industry, F. G. was determined to acquire it somehow. He turned for help to an old friend and creditor, Col. C. C. Slaughter.

As early as the 1880s C. C. Slaughter was probably the largest cattleman in Texas. He was also one of the first in the state to experiment in large scale crossbreeding of Durham cattle with longhorns. F. G. and Slaughter had known each other since the days of the old Jumbo Ranch on the Double Mountain Fork. Slaughter's enormous Long S range bordered on the southwest. In appearance and bearing the two men were opposites: Slaughter was short, heavy-set, bearded, and flamboyant; F. G. was tall, slim, soft-spoken. But in many ways

[19] Hodges, "Memoirs."

they were cut from the same cloth. Each had known the hardships of Civil War and Reconstruction, calamities that nearly wrecked their families. Both had trailed cattle to Kansas and later had moved west as pioneer ranchers. Tough, adaptable, both knew how to win against long odds. They were shrewd, these two, the type who recognized fortunes where others saw only barren waste or arid landscapes. By the mid-1890s the two veteran cattle barons were ready once again to make their mark.

In Slaughter's hometown of Dallas, F. G. explained what had happened in West Texas, how he could not afford the Goodnight herd, but why it was a wise investment. Slaughter was intrigued with the idea of owning the cattle, but he had no pasture available where they wouldn't mix with Durhams and longhorns. F. G. suggested that the cattle could graze on his own land; much of it was already divided into fenced pasture. For years, F. G. had been fencing his range, hauling in cedar posts and barbed wire from Colorado City; more than a hundred miles of fences now crossed his ranges. In exchange for pasturing the Goodnight cattle, F. G. asked for one quarter of the herd and half of the calf crop at the end of four years. Slaughter accepted. He purchased the herd sight unseen for fifty thousand dollars. If F. G. Oxsheer considered these cattle the best, there could be no doubt.[20]

They placed the Goodnight cattle on the original Oxsheer ranch, F. G.'s finest on the Staked Plains. No sooner were the animals driven through the gates, however, than the two men took steps to improve the herd. Buying prize-winning cattle from farms in Missouri, Iowa, and Illinois, Slaughter added fifty-seven of the "best bulls in America," including Ancient Briton, the grand champion of the 1893 Chicago World's Fair. Slaughter was so excited that he persuaded F. G. to name the ranch the Ancient Briton. At the same time, F. G. obtained registered bulls descended from another grand champion, Anxiety the Fourth, and from the old Swan Cattle Company, once the greatest ranch in Wyoming. Soon an incredible number of award-winning animals were on the Llano Estacado, grazing on the land of F. G. Oxsheer. The purchases by F. G. and Slaughter, the sheer quantity of prized

---

[20] C. C. Slaughter to F. G. Oxsheer, Letter of Agreement, July 9, 1898, Oxsheer Family Papers; David J. Murrah, *C. C. Slaughter: Rancher, Banker, Baptist*, p. 76.

stock they acquired, amazed cattle breeders everywhere. The dramatic entry of so many registered Hereford cattle into the Southwest marked a turning point in the American cattle industry. West Texas was no longer a land of only yucca plants and longhorns—it was also home of the largest and finest herd of Herefords in the United States, if not the world.[21]

In the fall of 1899 F. G. Oxsheer was nearly fifty years old. Riding down the Cap Rock on a crisp, sunny afternoon, he looked forward to the days ahead when he would be with the family celebrating his birthday. Everyone would be there: Mary and the children, friends, neighbors, distant kin. Mary would have a white carnation tied to his chair at the head of the table. The entire celebration would go on for a day or two—birthdays were always special in the Oxsheer home. But as he followed the switchbacks to the plains below, thinking of the fun ahead, he could not help but reflect on the past as well. It had all happened so quickly. In the late 1880s he had been struggling to survive, hanging on through disastrous weather and financial calamity with a small herd and a few windmills. Six years later he had emerged as one of the major cattlemen of the Southwest, controlling nearly one and a quarter million acres and owning outright more than twenty-five thousand head of stock. Six years more and he owned some of the finest beef cattle in America. Across the nation his name was linked with the best in registered stock. Like his father before him, F. G. was now "Colonel Oxsheer." Wherever he rode men doffed their Stetsons, smiling ladies curtsied and sometimes looked twice at the handsome figure with the graying sideburns.[22]

It also seemed only yesterday that he was a young man in Calvert and the children were babies. Mabel, the oldest, was now married and

---

[21] Hodges, "Memoirs"; F. G. Oxsheer, Personal Memo, Mar. 2, 1900, Oxsheer Family Papers; C. C. Comstock to F. G. Oxsheer, Sept. 16, 1898, Oxsheer Family Papers; Murrah, *C. C. Slaughter*, p. 76.

[22] The number of stock is a conservative estimate based on interviews, analysis of land holdings, and courthouse documents that occasionally refer to the Oxsheer herds. Even after the calamitous blizzards of 1885-86, for example, records show the half-million-acre Jumbo Cattle Company with more than sixteen thousand cattle. Deed Records, vol. 3, pp. 302-306; Mitchell County Courthouse, Colorado City, Tex.; Hodges, "Memoirs"; W. A. Oxsheer, interview; Mrs. Frank Miller, interview with the author, Gail, Tex., Oct. 11, 1983.

A Cattleman's Legacy

soon no doubt would have children of her own. The other girls, Myrtle and Beal, were only a few years younger. F. G., Jr. was working on the ranches and taking part in their management. The younger boys, Drennan and Coke, were still children, but already they wanted to be cowmen like their father. Some day all of the boys would ride at his side across a ranching empire that would be their legacy. What a stirring thought—it was one that made all of the hard work worthwhile.[23]

[23] Family Bible, Oxsheer Family Papers; Hodges, "Memoirs."

CHAPTER V

Revolutions

On a blustery evening in the early 1900s, a cowboy stepped from his dugout at the Ancient Briton Ranch. Clutching the brim of his hat, he stared into the gusting wind, scanning the plains. The winds had raged for nearly a week, raising clouds of dust and sand that cut his face like sleet, but every night the cowboy had kept vigil: watching, waiting, hoping his luck would hold. This night what he saw filled him with dread. Miles to the southwest the sky was an angry red, growing brighter by the minute. Soon he could see the outline of flames. The horizon was dancing with fire.

Roused by the man's shout, a dozen cowboys, buttoning their shirts or buckling their belts, burst from nearby dugouts. Some raced to the corral and saddled horses; a few heaved water barrels onto a wagon, hitched up a team of mules, and drove to the water trough. Others carried gunnysacks, wagon sheets, tarpaulins, and saddle blankets—anything they could find to beat out burning grass. Within minutes all were in the wagon or on horseback, racing toward the fire.

As they neared the blaze, the men met cattle, antelope, jackrabbits, and coyotes, all racing wildly away from the fire. Two riders roped and killed a steer, cut it open from throat to tail, then broke the ribs so the carcass would lie flat on the flesh side. They fastened their ropes to the dead animal's hind legs and began dragging it over the flames. Other cowboys jumped from the wagon to beat out the blaze with wet sacks. While a man on the wagon handed down wet sacks, the rest stamped out the flames that skipped over the blood-soaked grass. It was desperate work fighting prairie fires, a desperation born of ancient, instinctive fears.

They fought for hours, but the great wall of flame raged on, shifting directions with the wind and leaping swiftly ahead, blackening thousands of acres. It was dawn before the blaze finally burned itself out and the weary men rode back to camp, too exhausted to wash or even eat. Faces black with soot, hair and eyebrows singed, most of them simply collapsed in their dugouts for a few hours' rest, knowing in their hearts they had lost the struggle. F. G. Oxsheer's finest pasture had been destroyed.[1]

Prairie fire was terrifying, but in a sense it was also an omen of bad times ahead. With the turn of the century unwanted changes swept like flames across the Llano Estacado, destroying the old ways and ushering in the new. Railroads had come first, bringing barbed wire and windmills to F. G. and others like him. Now the railroads brought the other agents of change—farmers with their steel plows. They arrived by the hundreds, then by the thousands, until it seemed they would overrun the plains. Tanned, lank men along with haggard, determined women and towheaded offspring, they promised to alter the land forever by sheer numbers. Since Jamestown the pattern had been the same: first trappers and Indian traders, then cattlemen, and finally the farmers pushing all before them.[2]

Adding to the problem was the government in Austin. With the closing of the frontier, farmer-oriented legislators began altering land laws in a way that would have pleased the most ardent Jacksonian Democrats. Public leases to West Texas cattlemen were canceled and their ranges opened to settlement in small tracts. Overnight, ranchers

[1] Frances Hodges, "Memoirs," in possession of the W. A. Oxsheer family, Fort Worth, Tex.

[2] To encourage settlers, Texas had been generous in the disposition of its public land. Millions of acres were given away through Spanish, Mexican, Republic of Texas, and state land grants. By 1884 the state had given the railroads thirty-seven million acres, allotting the land in alternate sections like a checkerboard. Railroads received odd-numbered sections; the state retained the others. When cattlemen like F. G. Oxsheer pushed west, they bought or leased sections of railroad land and in time fenced the alternate public sections along with their own, often without leasing them. In semiarid West Texas, cattle raising required large unbroken land tracts. Thus when farmers scrambled for the last bits of state land in the 1890s, they found much of it fenced and claimed by ranchers. The result was a massive conflict of interests between cattlemen determined to maintain their pastures and farmers eager to purchase low-cost state land. Don H. Biggers, "From Cattle Range to Cotton Patch," *Frontier Times* 21, no. 4 (Jan., 1944): 206; R. D. Holt, "Cattlemen and Settlers 'Rushed' for School Land," *The Cattleman* 21 (Aug., 1934): 20; W. C. Holden, "The Problem of Maintaining the Solid Range on the Spur Ranch," *Southwestern Historical Quarterly* 34, no. 1 (July, 1930): 2.

who had leased state property since the 1880s were in danger of losing entire sections of their pastures to "nesters."[3]

The fools, cattlemen raged, the fools in wagons and the fools in Austin, didn't they understand? The plains were not East Texas, Kentucky, or Georgia. In the West a man couldn't scratch a living from 160 acres; he would starve first, or more likely, dry up and scatter with the wind. It hadn't occurred to them yet that ranchers had already shown a way. Thanks to windmills, cattlemen like F. G. Oxsheer had proved that farming as well as ranching was possible in West Texas. Across the plains ranchers found prospective settlers stalking across their pastures, carelessly starting prairie fires, leaving gates open, and even butchering cattle. Soon nesters began building homes, plowing the soil, and turning their milk cows loose to mix with ranchers' blooded stock. Everywhere, it seemed, cattlemen stumbled over plowed ground and property stakes.

At first, ranchers fought back, stampeding herds over crops or swooping down on farms in moonlight raids that often ended in floggings or even death. Some fenced around nester claims, hoping to isolate them. Others tried to maneuver around new laws that limited public land sales to four sections per man. F. G. Oxsheer loaned money to family, friends, and ranch hands so they could file on state land inside his ranch boundaries. Once they acquired the property, they signed over the title deeds to him. On mornings when public tracts opened for sale, bow-legged cowboys lined up in front of courthouse doors, jostling with farmers who had also come to file claims. At the Borden County Courthouse in Gail, cowhands from the Jumbo Cattle Company and surrounding ranches wore blue ribbons to distinguish friend from nester. When the doors opened, the line turned into a mob: fistfights, men clutching one another as they rolled on the floor, everyone scrambling for land. Some walked on the bodies of the struggling mass to reach the door; others crawled on hands and knees. The Jumbo cowboys were sorry that Turk was no longer with them. He would have been handy that morning.[4]

[3] In 1901 the Texas legislature revised the law that evicted cattlemen from state land before their leases had expired. But the revision merely postponed the inevitable. As soon as ranch leases expired, public lands were opened for settlement. David Murrah, *C. C. Slaughter: Rancher, Banker, Baptist*, pp. 84, 104.

[4] Memo on Land Claims, F. G. Oxsheer, July 15, 1901, Oxsheer Family Papers, Fort Worth, Tex.; Deed Title Transfer, J. P. Stokes to F. G. Oxsheer, Feb. 14, 1902, Mar-

It was desperate, but hopeless. Cattlemen could no more check the westward migration than could the Comanches. Ranchers might weather droughts and blizzards and survive money panics, but they couldn't keep farmers from the land. By the early 1900s cattlemen were a minority in West Texas. It became impossible to get favorable decisions on matters of trespass or even rustling from nester juries. Pastures were converted into fields and settlements; property values—and property taxes—mounted steadily. Men like F. G. Oxsheer who had grazed cattle on more than a million acres lost the ranges they did not own. The old Jumbo Cattle Company simply folded. Driven from the range by homesteaders, Jumbo cowboys could do nothing but sabotage the wells, filling them with cedar posts and rocks before they rode away.[5]

In 1900 F. G. Oxsheer bowed to the inevitable. He decided to leave the Llano Estacado and rebuild away from the influx of nesters. He began selling major portions of his range to farmers, small ranchers, realtors, or anyone else with cash. One large tract went for $121,000 to the cereal magnate C. W. Post, who planned to cut it into small farms. But the best land went to an old friend and business partner, C. C. Slaughter.[6]

They had done well together, F. G. and Slaughter, building cattle empires and award-winning herds, but the time had come to part. Slaughter was not yet convinced that big ranching was finished on the Staked Plains, and was determined to have one last try. He offered F. G. a generous commission to help him piece together another ranch. From neighboring cattlemen and in-laws as well as public land sales, F. G. acquired nearly 300,000 acres for Slaughter's Lazy S Ranch. The last portion of the Lazy S came from F. G.'s own Ancient Briton Ranch—40,000 acres called the "west pasture."

---

tin County, Tex., Oxsheer Family Papers; Deed title transfer, E. L. Barrows to F. G. Oxsheer, July 10, 1903, Hockley County, Tex., Oxsheer Family Papers; State Land Certificate no. 2507, Application of Mary Oxsheer, Mar. 13, 1903, Howard and Glasscock counties, Tex., Oxsheer Family Papers; Robert Beal, interview with the author, Fort Worth, Tex., June 30, 1983.

[5] Mr. and Mrs. W. H. Jones to Jeff Townsend, Aug. 15, 1972, Interview, Oral History File, Southwest Collection, Texas Tech University, Lubbock, Tex.

[6] Oil was discovered on much of this land in 1937, the enormous Slaughter oil field. By the end of 1975 total production had reached 642,687,368 barrels, or an approximate income to the landowners of twenty million dollars per year. Financial memo, F. G. Oxsheer, Dec. 28, 1906, Oxsheer Family Papers; Murrah, *C. C. Slaughter*, p. 134.

The two cattlemen met on the open plains to close the deal. F. G. was at a chuckwagon with some of his men when Slaughter rode up. At first the two friends sat around the campfire with the cowboys, saying little as they enjoyed a noon meal. Later, F. G. and Slaughter walked away from the others to talk. They spoke of old days and changing times, then reviewed their agreement and, typical of their breed, shook hands. With that handshake forty thousand acres changed owners. No papers or contracts were involved, no lawyers standing at one's side feigning interest for clients in exchange for legal fees, nothing but the word of two men and a handshake. For either to have asked for anything more would have been an insult.[7]

In a few minutes, F. G. went back to the chuckwagon and his cook, Hiley Boyd. "I just sold out to Slaughter," he announced, "land, wagons, teams, the men too, if that suits them." Hiley winked, thinking his boss was teasing again, but F. G. went on. "I told Slaughter about you, Boyd. He wants to make you foreman; if I were you I'd take the job. He'll pay you more than I can." Still Hiley said nothing. "You can stay with me if you like; I'll be glad to have you. Boyd, you're as good a man as I've got, but there's your future." F. G. was pointing toward Slaughter. Finally the young man realized F. G. was serious. Hiley thanked him for his honesty, shook hands, then walked over to his new boss.[8]

Hiley Boyd went on to become foreman and later a cowman on his own. The Lazy S was C. C. Slaughter's last great venture in the cattle business, however. Securing vast land tracts was only part of the problem facing large-scale ranching. Confronted with mounting operating costs and shrinking profits, Slaughter turned increasingly to real estate, banking, and insurance in the years ahead. For F. G. Oxsheer, on the other hand, there would be no turning from the only life he had known since he was nineteen. He left the country he had pioneered, but not the cattle business. In the early 1900s he began piecing together another ranching empire, starting far to the south, in a land without nesters, in another country—almost another world—Chihuahua, Mexico.

In 1900 Mexico was a blend of the old ways and the new, just as the population was a mixture of Spanish and Indian. Under the iron

---

[7] Hiley Boyd, Jr., interview with the author, Lubbock, Tex., June 13, 1983.
[8] Hiley Boyd, Jr., interview.

hand of Porfirio Díaz the government had pressed for the development of railroads as well as mining, public utilities, and ranching. What was happening was akin to the forming of industrial empires in the United States, but in Mexico the rules were those of the old Spanish system, the hacienda.

Maybe there was something from his boyhood on Little River that drew F. G. to Mexico, a half-remembered life of great estates and servile labor. The hacienda was more than a Mexican ranch, it was a way of life—what the Old South might have become had it survived. Under this system the peon was at the mercy of the landed *hacendado*, who assigned fields to work or cattle to tend, allocated punishment and reward, rest and labor. Many *hacendados* were decent men who took a paternal interest in their peons; others regarded them as animals, but everywhere the pattern was the same. The peon, supposedly free, was always a humble servant, hat in hand.

Field crops and range stock furnished food. The hacienda store—*la tienda de raya*—was the source of supply. Improvements came from available resources: homemade plows drawn by homegrown oxen; wooden, hand-carved harrows; rawhide instead of nails. The purpose of owning land was social as well as economic. Holding vast acres meant prestige and power.

A peon had a legal right to a few pesos a month, several pecks of corn, and a little garden, but he spent every peso at the hacienda store. If he ran short of money before the end of the month, he borrowed against future wages. Once he was in debt there was no hope of escape, and the size of the debt made no difference. It was merely a symbol of his condition in life and part of the legacy a father left his son.

Among this impoverished mass there was one group of men, however, who rivaled even the *hacendado* in dignity, freedom of movement, and self-respect—the vaqueros. For more than three centuries vaqueros had lived on the Mexican frontier, eking out a poor but unchained life with horses and cattle. In a country where individuals were valued for their hardiness and skill, these men were more than peons on horseback. They had struggled against nature and fought Indians and bandits as they ranged over the vast haciendas. Their values, methods, and even clothing had become standardized long before families like the Oxsheers crossed the Blue Ridge Mountains in the 1700s. Wide sombreros with peaked crowns, broad leather belts with silver buckles, buckskin jackets and tough canvaslike pants, half-boots, cowhide chaps, and colorful serapes thrown over the shoulders all marked a genuine native costume. Their food was chili peppers and beans, tortillas and beef, chorizo and roasted kid. Their language was Spanish, but the working vocabulary—*corral, bronco, loco, lazo, la reata, adobe, pinto, rancho*—spread far beyond their own world. On the haciendas of frontier Mexico evolved the cowboy lifestyle that would leave its stamp across the American West.

In 1901 F. G. Oxsheer bought the Hacienda de Sainapuchic from another American, E. W. Gould, Jr., nephew of the railroad magnate Jay Gould. Sixty miles west of Chihuahua City, the vast estate spread for miles across rolling pastures and fields of corn, beans, and sugarcane. More than four hundred peons lived on the land. Along the western boundary rose the Sierra Madre, mountains so vast and rugged they had remained largely unexplored, even in the twentieth century. To the north and east stretched the Chihuahua Plains—the heart of Sainapuchic and some of the finest ranch land in northern Mexico.[9]

At the foot of the mountains on a tree-shaded knoll stood the hacienda headquarters—a sprawling, fortresslike structure built around a courtyard. The exterior was plain and dingy, almost prisonlike, with plastered adobe walls. Beauty was reserved for the interior: a courtyard, fountains, hanging plants, and a projecting tile roof supported by hand-carved Corinthian pillars. The door of every room opened onto the courtyard; the walls were thick and solid to keep out winter chill and summer heat that often rose above a hundred degrees. Supporting the roof were enormous wooden beams, hewn from the forests of the Sierra Madre.[10]

Dozens of men dressed in white cotton pants, faded blue shirts, and straw sombreros trudged through the fields behind oxen and plows. Farther away on the distant plain vaqueros watched the cattle. In shadowed, walled patios of nearby stables were the red embers of blacksmith forges and sooty figures pounding hot metal into tools, hardware, and horseshoes. Beyond the quadrangle of feeding troughs and work-

[9] Hodges, "Memoirs"; F. G. Oxsheer, Jr., to Mary Oxsheer, July 17, 1901, Oxsheer Family Papers; J. S. Pawley to F. G. Oxsheer, Nov. 29, 1905, Oxsheer Family Papers; C. W. Powers to F. G. Oxsheer, May 23, 1901, Oxsheer Family Papers; Hand-drawn maps of Hacienda de Sainapuchic, ca. 1901–1902, Oxsheer Family Papers.

[10] Hand-drawn maps of Hacienda de Sainapuchic, ca. 1901–1902, Oxsheer Family Papers; Financial report, May 7, 1901, Oxsheer Family Papers.

shops were stone corrals. The crack of whips and shouts of plodding beasts, bareback porters bent double under towering loads, barefoot women cooking, cleaning, and sewing in the master's home—it was part of an ageless, inherited pattern.[11]

The peons inhabited stick huts with thatched roofs. Inside were pallets for beds and a few other hand-hewn items. In a corner was usually a small altar and warped candle; outside hung potted plants and bird cages. At twilight, when chores were done and cool air swept down from the mountains, life flowed back into the little homes. Groups of whiskered men squatted in the shadows, smoking corn-husk cigarettes and talking. Inside, women crouched in the glow of cook fires, stirring pots of beans or patting tortillas. Scrawny dogs and grimy youngsters scampered back and forth across the yards; adolescent boys strolled about seeking romance. After darkness settled on Sainapuchic sometimes a guitar was heard, gently pouring out a haunting melody of forsaken love or hopeless plight. Nighttime cloaked a thousand injustices bred by the hacienda system.[12]

F. G. Oxsheer in Mexico is the story of innovation and a cattleman's savvy. Soon after acquiring Sainapuchic, he fired the superintendent, the clerk, and several of the foremen, recognizing them as drunkards and incompetents. To modernize and expand beef-raising potential, he put in windmills and stock tanks, strung barbed wire, and imported large numbers of registered Herefords and Holsteins. Just as on the Staked Plains of Texas, F. G. was one of the first in Mexico to raise Hereford cattle. So great was his reputation as a breeder of blooded stock, he was soon named general manager of the Mexican Hereford Breeding and Importing Company, a group of American investors with holdings in Mexico. One of them, Frank Rockefeller, considered him one of the most brilliant cattlemen in North America. The wisest and most far-reaching of F. G.'s many decisions, however, involved the selection of the new superintendent—his son, F. G., Jr.[13]

[11] Inventory of stock in Sainapuchic store, Aug. 4, 1901, Oxsheer Family Papers.

[12] General ledger balances, Sept. 8, 1901, Oxsheer Family Papers; H. F. Smith to F. G. Oxsheer, May 17, 1908, Oxsheer Family Papers.

[13] E. W. Gould, Jr. to F. G. Oxsheer, Nov. 27, 1901, Mobile, Ala., Oxsheer Family Papers; J. Warren to F. G. Oxsheer, Oct. 30, 1907, Oxsheer Family Papers; C. W. Powers to F. G. Oxsheer, June 7, 1901, Oxsheer Family Papers; H. F. Smith to F. G. Oxsheer, May 17, 1908, Oxsheer Family Papers; Pamphlet of Mexican Hereford Breeding and Importing Company, n.d., Chillicothe, Mo., Oxsheer Family Papers.

F. G., Jr. was only twenty years old when his father put him in charge of Sainapuchic. Tall, striking in appearance, he often dressed in tailored suits like his dad, wore monogrammed silk shirts and hand-fashioned boots with "gal-leg" spurs. In a way he was a deeply troubled young man, driven by an inner need to equal or outperform his father; but he was also brilliant, perhaps a genius. As a child he memorized an entire book on French etiquette as a guide for social behavior. More important, along the way he also mastered the most intricate financial concepts and developed an almost instinctive understanding of human nature. He never attended college; for him it would have been a waste of time. As ranch superintendent and bookkeeper, he converted Sainapuchic into a model ranching enterprise.[14]

When the Oxsheers bought Sainapuchic, the hacienda was operating at an annual loss of nearly eight thousand dollars. Within two years F. G., Jr. was producing a profit. Word of his success spread, and soon men came from neighboring haciendas to see for themselves. California senator George Hearst sent men from his own million-acre Mexican ranch, Babricora, to study the Oxsheer methods. The Zuloagas, a ranching family for generations and the proud descendants of Mexican governors and presidents, were so impressed they ultimately formed a limited partnership, buying a share of the Oxsheer ranch.[15]

One of the Oxsheer secrets was the way F. G., Jr. worked with the peons. Unlike most Americans in Mexico, he had the good sense to learn the language and customs. Instead of belittling the culture, he accepted it and worked to build a ranch with what was available. When a vaquero was injured or ill, he brought the man into the main house to be cared for until he recovered. If land needed fencing and no tools were available, he simply made do, ordering postholes dug with crowbars and bare hands. In F. G., Jr. the peons found someone that all their traditions and history had taught them to revere, the great patrón—powerful, flamboyant, outwardly self-assured. Even in Chihuahua City men heard of him and were impressed. Abraham González, for instance, a cattle broker and political leader, soon counted F. G., Jr.

[14] Billy Oxsheer, interview with the author, Fort Worth, Tex., June 22, 1983; C. W. Powers to F. G. Oxsheer, May 24, 1901, Oxsheer Family Papers; F. G. Oxsheer, Jr. to F. G. Oxsheer, June 3, 1901, Oxsheer Family Papers.

[15] General ledger balances, Sept. 8, 1901, Oxsheer Family Papers; General ledger balances, June 10, 1903, Oxsheer Family Papers; C. W. Powers to F. G. Oxsheer, July 4, 1901, Oxsheer Family Papers; J. S. Pawley to F. G. Oxsheer, Nov. 1, 1905, Oxsheer Family Papers.

among his friends. The time would come when the Oxsheers would have need of a friend like Abraham González.[16]

Another "associate" of F. G., Jr.'s was a wily figure named Doroteo Arango, better known as Pancho Villa. His father never knew the details, but F. G., Jr. was in touch with Villa within a year after arriving in Mexico. The two could have met through Abraham González or peons at Sainapuchic. However it happened, Villa and F. G., Jr. quickly recognized that each had something to offer the other.[17]

For years Pancho Villa had lived in the Sierra Madre west of Sainapuchic with a band of several hundred men, swooping down on haciendas, killing and plundering, then retreating to his mountain stronghold. This was probably the reason E. W. Gould sold Sainapuchic to the Oxsheers. No one could stop these raids, but F. G., Jr. devised a way to protect his father's land. Instead of fighting bandits in a hopeless, no-win guerrilla war like other *hacendados*, he got in touch with their leader. The result was a secret understanding: in exchange for horses, food, and supplies, bandits would spare the Oxsheer ranch. For several years this shadowy relationship went on, Villa raiding with mounting ferocity, stripping haciendas of all their cattle, while Sainapuchic remained strangely untouched. There were rumors of men on horseback who came and went at night from the Oxsheer estate, but no one could prove these stories. All that could be said for sure was that Sainapuchic flourished in a time of mounting chaos and bloodshed.[18]

It was a daring little game, and dangerous. If authorities discovered what was happening, the Oxsheers were finished in Mexico; F. G., Jr. would be jailed. But if he sided against Villa, Sainapuchic would be destroyed. It took someone with audacity to pull it off. If his father had known what was going on, he probably would have sold the ranch and yanked his son out of the country.

While F. G, Jr., did his juggling act in Mexico, hundreds of miles to the north his father was busy with other matters. When F. G. Ox-

[16] The information on Abraham González comes from memos scribbled on the back of a business card found in the old Oxsheer home in Fort Worth, Tex. This source is cited hereafter as Business card; C. W. Powers to F. G. Oxsheer, May 23, 1901, Oxsheer Family Papers; C. W. Powers to F. G. Oxsheer, July 4, 1901, Oxsheer Family Papers; F. G. Oxsheer, Jr. to F. G. Oxsheer, June 3, 1901, Oxsheer Family Papers.

[17] Billy Oxsheer, interview.

[18] Billy Oxsheer, interview; J. E. Oxsheer, interview with the author, Fort Worth, Tex., Aug. 9, 1983.

sheer left the Staked Plains, he bought more than a Mexican hacienda; he acquired an entire ranching network to replace what he had sold. In Glasscock, Howard, and Martin counties, F. G. established the Diamond Ranch, 200,000 acres on the southernmost extremity of the Llano Estacado. Of all the ranches he would own, the Diamond was his favorite. East of Lubbock he leased the Z Bar L Ranch in Crosby County, 120,000 acres, and in Jones County established another horse ranch. Finally, in the Trans-Pecos region of southwest Texas he built the Pecos Ranch, 70,000 acres, and the 23,000-acre Blanca Ranch.[19]

The last two, the Pecos and the Blanca ranches, were in some of the most isolated, inhospitable country in the United States. But this was precisely why the region appealed to F. G. Oxsheer: it was not a place that would attract large numbers of settlers—especially farmers. Even at the turn of the century the land west of the Pecos was in many ways as wild as the day settlers first arrived. Mustangs and longhorns roamed freely. Ocelots, jaguars, and mountain lions stalked the deserts, canyons, and mountains. The only signs of man were an occasional barbed-wire fence or windmill.[20]

The Trans-Pecos had long been a gathering place of Apache and Comanche raiders as well as Mexican and American bandits—a no-man's-land where the only friends were often a good horse or a gun. Only since the 1890s had a semblance of law and order come to the region. The land had an uninviting, hostile quality, for the Texas plains gave way to the desert west of the Pecos. It was a country of barren, chocolate-colored mountains, of cactus, scorpions, tarantulas, and dry alkaline lake beds. Evenings were generally cool, but daytime temperatures could soar above 115 degrees. At times, in this empty land, there was no rain for years.

After a roundup in this rugged country, horses' legs were gashed by cactus. The treacherous Spanish dagger—twelve inches long and

---

[19] The site of the Pecos Ranch was in present-day Pecos and Terrell counties. The Blanca Ranch was in present-day Hudspeth County. Hodges, "Memoirs"; Real estate advertisement of Pecos Ranch, ca. 1915, Oxsheer Family Papers; F. G. Oxsheer to J. H. Rawls, Blanca Ranch Contract of Sale, Mar. 31, 1920, Oxsheer Family Papers; Deed Records, vol. 67, p. 179, vol. 79, p. 122, Jones County Courthouse, Anson, Tex. Plat, Oxsheer Diamond Ranch, Howard, Martin, and Glasscock counties, Block no. 34, compiled by T. H. Seavy, June 28, 1913, in possession of Cy Marcus, Fort Worth, Tex.; W. A. Oxsheer, interview with the author, Fort Worth, Tex., July 6 and 7, 1983.

[20] Hodges, "Memoirs."

ending with needle-sharp points—could pierce the sole of an animal's foot. Coming down mountains, cowboys often had to jump their horses from ledges several feet high, sometimes landing in the middle of Spanish daggers. The men who worked this desert wore leather chaps and brush jackets even in midsummer. There was no other way to protect themselves from the brush and thorns.

There were no railroads or towns for marketing cattle near the Pecos and Blanca ranches. After the steer roundup every fall, F. G.'s men drove his herds to the railroad towns of Sanderson and Sierra Blanca. In some ways it was like the old days on the Chisholm Trail, but he had come a long way since he ate dust as a drag rider. Now in the early 1900s, F. G. Oxsheer possessed more than half a million acres and was one of the leading cattlemen of the United States and Mexico. Sixty-one years old in 1910, he was still fit and vigorous. He rode in front of the herds he sent to market, and of course, always wore a suit—usually last year's Sunday best. No matter how hot or dusty, he dressed as if riding to the governor's ball.[21]

Driving cattle under desert skies and building a second ranching empire, F. G. Oxsheer had again triumphed, but disaster was never far away. In 1910 another set of unexpected challenges and problems were destined to sweep the land. In Mexico and along the border a people and a nation were about to explode.

By 1910, a few thousand foreign investors and 3 percent of the native population owned virtually all of the arable land in Mexico, a country that had increased from nine million to fifteen million inhabitants in thirty years. Millions of landless Mexicans had nothing to do and no place to go. Human labor grew so cheap that it cost less to hire a man than a mule. Even on the best-managed estates, custom and economics often buried compassion. F. G. had wondered about it every time he visited Sainapuchic. No matter how much the peons smiled, no matter how friendly they appeared, there was always a lingering suspicion that behind those dark eyes lay a smoldering hatred.

The mortality rate in Mexico was almost triple that of Western Europe or the United States; the infant mortality rate exceeded that of

[21] Hodges, "Memoirs"; Mr. and Mrs. Sam Wilkinson to Bobby Weaver, Mar. 15, 1979, Interview, Oral History File, Southwest Collection, Texas Tech University, Lubbock, Tex. D. W. Cooper, interview with the author, Fort Worth, Tex., Sept. 21, 1983.

even China or India. Rampant alcoholism and the rising use of marijuana were symptoms of the misery; there was little else to ease the pain of life. But these ills, along with widespread illegitimacy, were condemned by the upper class as moral, not social problems. Under the Díaz regime millions struggled through life without hope.

As early as 1908 Pancho Villa advised F. G., Jr. to leave this troubled land. Growing numbers of desperate men were stealing and plundering to live, and Villa undoubtedly knew he could no longer guarantee the safety of Sainapuchic. Abraham González also warned of problems ahead and offered his services to the Oxsheers as cattle broker and realtor if they sold out. Possibly Villa and González were generalizing when they spoke of trouble in Mexico, but they might have had specific plans in mind—both were enemies of the Díaz regime. The Oxsheers wisely took their advice, and with the help of González shipped their cattle to Texas, then sold the hacienda in 1909[22] to a pair of brothers named Holly.

A few months later peons of the village of Cuchillo Parado lashed out at their oppressors in a running skirmish with the dreaded *rurales*, or rural police. Armed vaqueros under Pancho Villa swept down from the mountains in the San Andrés region, and Abraham González emerged as revolutionary governor of Chihuahua. The Mexican Revolution had begun. Panic-stricken American and European investors fled for their lives, but not everyone made it. The Holly brothers were killed by Villa's men before they could get away from Sainapuchic. Across the land, Mexico was soon ripped apart in a frenzy of bloodletting and anarchy that would last for ten years.[23]

At first the Mexican Revolution was little more than a topic of conversation for Texans, but this soon changed. Like most revolutions, the

---

[22] Billy Oxsheer, interview; Business card; Hodges, "Memoirs."

[23] Francisco J. Madero, whose family owned large haciendas in northern Mexico, "pronounced" against Porfirio Díaz in October, 1910, and called for an insurrection to begin on November 20. Violent outbreaks against the government occurred all over Mexico; in the north, Villa and others stole the haciendas' cattle and sold them in the United States in order to purchase weapons.

The army came to Sainapuchic to escort the Holly brothers to safety. The brothers were some distance from the ranch when they remembered valuable papers they had left behind in the office safe. They asked for an escort to return to the ranch, but it was refused, so they went back alone to get their papers. When they arrived at the hacienda, Villa's men were waiting for them. Hodges, "Memoirs."

one in Mexico began to exert an influence beyond its national boundaries. The real problem was the chaos that allowed bandits to loot, rob, and murder as pretended revolutionaries on both sides of the border. In Texas this meant the spread of guerrilla warfare all along the Rio Grande. Before the Mexican Revoluiton was over, more blood was spilled along the border than in any American conflict between Appomattox and World War I. This border war went almost unnoticed in the shadow of the great European conflict that soon followed, but for the people of South Texas, especially ranchers like F. G. Oxsheer, it was as serious as anything they had ever faced.

Adding to the problems were social conditions along the Rio Grande. In addition to Anglo-American society, another cultural heritage and value system existed in South Texas that every Mexican considered as valid as that of the English-speaking world. The Mexicans of Texas were no more interested in accepting Anglo-American culture than were the French-Canadians or the Comanche-Kiowa. South Texas was not a melting pot but a land of separate societies. When revolution broke out across the border, conditions were ripe for revival of a racial blood feud nearly as old as Texas.

As the Mexican government collapsed, the situation on the border resembled the Comanche frontier half a century earlier. Large parties of Mexican raiders, occasionally aided by Texas Mexicans, rode into the state, looting and murdering. Just as quickly, Texas Rangers and sheriffs' posses struck back with a vengeance, killing Mexican nationals and Mexican-Americans, sometimes innocent and guilty alike. By 1915 hundreds of Anglo and Mexican farms and ranches in Texas had been hit, including F. G. Oxsheer's. Cattle and horses were stolen, homes burned, ranch hands and entire families killed or carried off, never to be heard from again. Throughout the border country men spoke of the "war zone" as thousands fled, leaving everything behind. No one knows how many died in this border conflict—estimates vary from five hundred to five thousand—but of the ferocity and venom displayed there can be no doubt.

A typical incident occurred near F. G. Oxsheer's Blanca Ranch on Christmas Day, 1917. It was early morning, and no one in the Sam Neil family expected trouble. The children were still sleeping; presents lay beneath the Christmas tree waiting to be unwrapped. It seemed like any other Christmas morning at the little ranch, but it wasn't. Sam Neil was looking out the kitchen window when he saw them. Coming up the road fast were forty or fifty men on horseback. As they came closer, he could see the unmistakable forms: the peak-topped sombreros, the ammunition belts strung across shoulders—they were bandits.

Neil raced into another room and grabbed his carbine, opened the front door and stepped onto the porch. The men on horseback were swarming about the ranch. One of them rode into the front yard, jerked his horse up, and shouted orders: "Kill all the Americans." They were his last words. Neil raised his carbine and fired, dropping the bandit with a single shot. The other men leaped from their horses and took cover behind adobe walls and dirt piles. Seconds later they were pouring in a murderous fire at Neil. They shot him, but he staggered back into the house and slammed the door. Other members of the family grabbed guns and rushed to the windows, shooting at anything that moved. They were hopelessly outnumbered, but those outside could not be sure. As long as the Neils kept up their fire, no one would rush the house.

The bandits tried to break the stalemate with a bluff. They ordered a surrender or they would dynamite the house, but the Neils were too experienced to be fooled. They knew the fate of anyone who surrendered to bandits. Next the Mexicans called a cease-fire, and for several hours all was quiet, at least until the stage arrived.[24]

Every afternoon a stagecoach stopped at the ranch to water the horses, and this day was no different. The driver, Mickey Welsh, pulled into the front yard before he realized what was happening. Some of the bandits rushed the stagecoach, opened the coach doors, and shot the passengers—two Mexicans. Others pulled Welsh off the stage and dragged him into a storehouse, slashed his throat, then pulled him up by a rope and left him twisting from a rafter. The bandits never forced their way into the Neils' home. They settled finally for plundering the storehouse and packing all they could on horses, then rode away toward mountains to the south. It had been a harrowing Christmas at the little ranch, but the episode was far from over.

A few months later Texas Rangers and a local posse trailed the same bandits to their village stronghold on the Rio Grande. Under

---

[24] U.S. Congress, Senate Committee on Foreign Relations, *Investigation of Mexican Affairs, Preliminary Report and the Hearings on S. Doc. 285*. 86th Cong., 2nd sess., 1920, vol. 1, p. 1526.

cover of night the Texans slipped into the village on foot, rounded up a number of suspects, then began marching away when someone shot at them from the brush. The Texans opened fire on everyone around them, prisoners as well as those in the brush. The next morning perhaps as many as fifteen Mexican bodies marked the site, another fifteen casualties in a vicious, undeclared war on the Texas border.[25]

As F. G. Oxsheer and his cowhands mended fences, branded cattle, or drove them to market, they were like soldiers facing combat, knowing that a brush with bandits would be a fight to the death. There was no way of knowing if over the next ridge fifty or a hundred bandits were waiting. The only thing to do when driving cattle was to stay in the open to avoid an ambush, and keep a loaded Colt .45 and carbine handy.[26]

Despite every effort, it became impossible for F. G. and other Texas cattlemen to protect their livestock from raiders. The ranges were vast and the raiders many and unpredictable. Again and again ranches in the Trans-Pecos were hit by bandits; some lost entire herds, others their lives. Faithful cowboys who had ridden for years at their bosses' sides now left the region to find safer work. For F. G. there was nothing to do but accept the inevitable. One man could not safeguard cattle scattered over nearly 100,000 acres. And he would not jeopardize the safety of F. G., Jr., or any of his sons by allowing them to help. In 1915 he sold the Pecos Ranch. Unable to find a buyer for the Blanca Ranch, he kept the land until 1920, but sold it at the first opportunity. As always, F. G. immediately sought new opportunities when forced to move. The thought of giving up ranching never crossed his mind.[27]

[25] Committee on Foreign Relations, *Investigations of Mexican Affairs*, vol. 1, pp. 1526, 1530–31.

[26] D. W. Cooper, interview; Hodges, "Memoirs."

[27] Hodges, "Memoirs"; Pecos Ranch Contract of Sale, Nov. 23, 1915, Oxsheer Family Papers; Blanca Ranch Contract of Sale, Mar. 31 1920, Oxsheer Family Papers.

CHAPTER VI

The Patriarch and His Flock

THE train raced east through the night, stopping briefly at Sweetwater, Baird, and Eastland. Set against the Texas plains, the coach cars dwindled into insignificance, mere beads of light moving across the dark, open landscape. Some of the passengers were in sleeping cars by midnight, but in the day coach at the end of the train the old man with the hearing horn remained awake. Turning away from the window he looked around at the half-empty coach, then stared at the vacant seat beside him, at his hearing horn and Stetson hat. Why did he have to be so old, he wondered. If he were younger he could still get financing for the ranch. These hard times would pass, like they always had. It would be different if Colonel Slaughter were still alive. Many times the Colonel had loaned him money, but those days were forever past. Colonel Slaughter and other friends and business associates were all gone now. This battle he must fight alone.[1]

The door at the front of the coach car opened and the old man looked up. A family stepped inside, probably from the last town. The husband and wife were middle-aged, the children—two boys and two girls—seemed to range from seven or eight to their early teens. The old man smiled faintly as he stared at them, for the oldest girl reminded him of one of his own daughters at that age: the same dark, flashing eyes and auburn hair. In a way the entire scene reminded him of something from his past. Nearly forty years ago he and Mary were middle-aged and taking their own family east on the same night train, on their way to a new home. It was not a hot September night like this one. Then it was cold and snowing. He remembered it well, recalling how thrilled his family had been on that train ride long ago, and how they sprang from their seats when the locomotive finally pulled into the station. It was a wonderfully exciting time. He was strong and healthy in those days, and one of the leading cattlemen of the Southwest. It was a season of his life filled

[1] Edwyna Thro, interview with the author, Wichita Falls, Tex., May 30, 1983.

with opportunities, successes, recognition, and gracious living. The new home was in Fort Worth, Texas. The year was 1895.[2]

Fort Worth was a bustling, upstart community in the mid-1890s. Electric lights lined paved streets filled with carriages, buggies, and mule-drawn trolley cars; a tangle of power lines crisscrossed a town of brick buildings, cattle pens, wood-framed shacks, and tree-shadowed mansions. The community was a mixture of the old and the new, of frontier and urban America, and it was fitting that F. G. Oxsheer should be a part of it. Perhaps no other town benefited more or longer from the beef cattle industry and the cattle barons. It began with the Chisholm Trail and continued with the stockyards and packing plants once the trail was closed. Earlier, Colorado City had been the cattlemen's capital in West Texas, and for eleven years the Oxsheers' home. But money panics, droughts, and a changing economy had put an end to Colorado City as a major beef marketing career. By the 1890s ranchers came from all over the state to sell their cattle and to build mansions in Fort Worth. They kept their far-flung ranches, but made their homes and headquarters in the fast-growing city on the Trinity River that reveled in the name "Cowtown."

The cattle business in Fort Worth was not the same as in the open country of the plains. Men didn't close deals around chuckwagons or campfires; they met at the stockyards, in hotel lobbies, or, by 1903, in the Exchange Building on the city's north side. Broad-shouldered men in dusty Stetsons and high-heeled boots mixed with dapper commission agents or fast-talking cattle brokers wearing derbies and buttoned shoes. The latest wire reports on beef prices in the Midwest or the East were discussed as much as range conditions along the Pecos River or the Double Mountain Fork. It was a mixture of Old West and turn-of-the-century styles typical of the entire city.

Some of the more important cattlemen, including F. G. Oxsheer, had offices but seldom used them. The chief place of business for cowmen was the downtown Metropolitan Hotel. Every morning F. G. met with commission agents or other cattlemen in the huge, red-carpeted

---

[2] John Drennan Oxsheer to Frances Hodges, Nov. 24, 1957, Oxsheer Family Papers, Fort Worth, Tex.; Frances Hodges, "Memoirs," in possession of the W. A. Oxsheer family, Fort Worth, Texas.

lobby, the coffee shop, or on the sidewalk in front of the hotel. He bought and sold thousands of cattle there over the years. Like most Fort Worth cattlemen, F. G. was away from town much of the time, tending to his herds and ranches in West Texas and Mexico. Countless times he took the train to Stanton, Big Spring, Lubbock, or Chihuahua, then exchanged coach car for horse and rode on, transformed again into a man of the plains. But whenever he was in Fort Worth, F. G. could usually be found at home or doing business at the Metropolitan.[3]

Shortly after the Oxsheers moved to Fort Worth, F. G. spent a day and most of a night at the Metropolitan Hotel. When it grew late, Mary became worried and sent a house servant to find him. Mary was long accustomed to her husband being away for days or even weeks; she knew he could handle himself on the range or in rowdy frontier towns. But Fort Worth was a "city" of more than twenty thousand, a place where new and unfamiliar dangers lurked. The servant returned with news. "Mr. Fount," he explained, "was on a big cattle deal and couldn't come home yet." Just before sunup F. G. finally stalked in, tired but smiling. He handed Mary a check for his night's work at the Metropolitan—ten thousand dollars.[4]

As soon as the Oxsheers arrived in Fort Worth, F. G. and Mary rented a small frame house and enrolled the children in school. The little house was cramped and uncomfortable in the winter chill, but they didn't stay there long. In the spring F. G. bought a home more in the style of a cattle baron, a spacious, two-story dwelling with clapboard siding, surrounded by oaks and pecan trees. An open-air porch extended across the front and one side of the home. The family often gathered on the porch in the evenings: F. G., Mary, and the children—Mabel, Myrtle, F. G., Jr., Coke, Drennan, and the youngest girl, Beal. It was a time for going over events of the day or plans for tomorrow, a time to strengthen family bonds. When it was hot, F. G. and Mary sometimes sipped a beer. Mary didn't like the beer, but she enjoyed sharing the time with her husband. Other evenings the couple merely sat together far into the night, just as they had years before on the porch of their first little home in Milam County.[5]

[3] Edwyna Thro, interview; Hodges, "Memoirs."
[4] Hodges, "Memoirs."
[5] Hodges, "Memoirs."

In the early 1900s the Oxsheers moved again to a larger and much finer home. In the course of his life F. G. would spend a fortune on himself and his family. Some would have called him vain and ostentatious. Perhaps they were right. But if these same people could have stood with F. G. as a boy, by his mother's sickbed when there was no money to pay for a doctor, they might have understood. No member of his family would ever again want for the material things of life if he could help it. On the southwest side of town, along a street lined with mansions belonging to the greatest cattle barons of Texas, he built a home that was in many ways a monument to all that he was.[6]

The great house rose two and a half stories from a foundation set in bedrock. The massive walls were gray brick; red Spanish tiles covered the roof, giving the dwelling a modified Georgian architectural style. Front steps led up to a broad, open-air porch supported by brick columns. Dark and stern in appearance, the home was actually bright and cheery inside, with more than eighty windows to let in the light. Upstairs were five bedrooms, and adjoining the master bedroom was a glass-enclosed porch. Downstairs was the parlor, sun room, and library with built-in bookshelves and cabinets, a pantry and kitchen, and finally, the dining room—the largest room in the house and the focal point of the home.

The furnishings and inlays were the finest money could buy. Imported Italian wallpaper, velvet drapes, walnut paneling, and recessed doors added to the elegance. A Betcheer tubing system served as an intercom to every room. Parlor and bedrooms were furnished in ornate Victorian style with reclining chairs, marble-top tables, and velour sofas. The parlor fireplace even had an onyx mantel. The sun room contained rattan furniture and enormous brass vases that Mary kept filled with ferns or fresh cuttings from the garden. A grand piano stood in the middle of the library. In the dining room was a huge mahogany table and chairs; on the table were sterling silver flatware, Haviland china, crystal ware, and monogrammed Irish linens from Walpole's of New York. The Oxsheers were not a family to quibble over costs. Pile carpets covered white oak and maple floors; crystal chandeliers hung

---

[6] John Drennan Oxsheer to Frances Hodges, Nov. 24, 1957, and Oct. 24, 1964, Oxsheer Family Papers; Edwyna Thro, interview; W. A. Oxsheer, interview with the author, Fort Worth, Tex., July 6 and 7, 1983.

from the elevated ceilings, and over the staircase was an enormous stained glass window.[7]

Behind the home stood servants' quarters. There were always five or six house servants at the mansion. Most of them were blacks, and several remained with the Oxsheers for years. There was one white servant, however, that the family never forgot. Mary hired a German immigrant as a cook. Cheerful and hard-working, she possessed but a single flaw—she could not communicate in English. Soon after she arrived, Mary told the woman to cook a pot of beans. Showing her a handful of pintos, then pointing to the stove, she was certain the woman understood. She didn't. Left alone in the kitchen, the new cook lugged from the cupboard a hundred-pound sack of beans that was meant for one of the ranches. She found a large iron pot in the backyard, built a fire, filled the pot with beans, then stepped back inside. When Mary returned she found a smiling cook, but nothing on the stove. Glancing out a window, however, she spotted something in the backyard: a steaming washtub erupting beans.[8]

In back of the servants' quarters were stables, a large barn, and gardens filled with vegetables that could grow in Texas. Beyond the garden was a vacant lot where F. G. kept two cows, at least until city hall forced him to remove them. He thought it was a lot of nonsense, forcing people to buy milk in cans or bottles, but he had no choice and shipped the cows back to the ranch. Shrubs and flowers were part of the landscaping. Surrounding the home and outbuildings was a brick fence with a wrought-iron front gate left open to welcome any visitor who cared to call. Finally, buried on the grounds or perhaps in the walls of the home was a small fortune in gold, a reserve set aside for emergencies.[9]

The Oxsheer mansion was more than buried treasure and expensive furniture. Day and night the great house rang with laughter, singing, and chatter. In addition to the family, there were usually relatives, business associates, friends, and acquaintances on hand. Every eve-

---

[7] The onyx mantel was ultimately replaced with one of marble. Edwyna Thro, interview; W. A. Oxsheer, interview.

[8] W. A. Oxsheer, interview; Hodges, "Memoirs."

[9] The gold has never been accounted for. I believe F. G. Oxsheer spent it in the last years of his life. Nothing remains today but the old home. The outbuildings and fence were torn down years ago, and much of the yard has been cut away to widen the street. Hodges, "Memoirs"; W. A. Oxsheer, interview.

ning twenty or thirty people gathered around the great mahogany dining table. One never knew who might be at either side when sitting down for a meal. The guests might be other cattle barons from West Texas, local business moguls such as Amon Carter and Sid Richardson, or in later years a budding movie star—Gary Cooper. Over the years guests came and went by the hundreds, but one thing remained constant—the open-handed hospitality of the host. He sat at the head of the table carving the meat, a table that groaned under the weight of hams, pork roasts, beef, chicken, vegetables, cornbreads, fried pies—and biscuits. F. G. loved hot biscuits and had a special floor pedal by his chair to summon the servant with more hot biscuits. There was always food enough for any number who came to his door, and guests were always welcome.[10]

Many times relatives came in the fall to shop in Fort Worth but stayed until warm weather the following spring. Some, like Cousin Jennie, remained for months at a time because they had nowhere else to stay. The Oxsheer residence was Cousin Jennie's retirement home, yet to F. G., she was as welcome as anyone. On summer afternoons she could be found on the front porch rocking peacefully, dipping snuff, and doing needlepoint. F. G.'s children often laughed about the "Oxsheer Hotel" and deplored the way some took advantage of their father's generosity, but never in his presence.[11]

There was apparently no limit to his generosity. He bought the two-story clapboard home where his family had lived before and relocated it to a vacant lot beside the mansion to serve as a guest house for the multitude of visitors. He repeatedly "loaned" money to friends who never repaid him. He sent the sons of former family slaves to college in the north, and when they returned, helped establish them in businesses of their own. Once F. G. received a letter for help from someone he had not seen in years—it was Kate, the orphaned servant who had worked for the Oxsheers long ago. She lived in the town of Sweetwater and was desperate. Her husband had lost his job, but even more serious, the Ku Klux Klan was threatening to run them off or worse. F. G. took the first train to Sweetwater, found Kate's husband a job, then looked up the local bully boys. Kate and her family were old friends of his, he told the Ku Klux; they were not to be harmed. Any-

---

[10] Hodges, "Memoirs"; W. A. Oxsheer, interview; Edwyna Thro, interview.
[11] Hodges, "Memoirs."

one bothering the family in any way would have to deal with him. They got the message. It was F. G.'s first and last encounter with the Klan.[12]

The Ku Klux, renegades, politicians and gunslingers, droughts and blizzards—F. G. Oxsheer saw these as one and the same—the enemies of civilization, the savages, the takers and destroyers. All of his life he fought them. He believed it his duty to set an example of gracious conduct and hospitality, give sound advice, and share home and fortune with those who surrounded him. He strived to hold up to his family and friends the highest possible standards of behavior and somehow get them all through the Pearly Gates. From the depths of his soul he believed that all that separated man from beast was Divine Providence and determination to live by a certain code no matter what the cost. Work, honesty, a sense of duty, and self-reliance, mixed with charity and compassion: this was F. G. Oxsheer's code. He was nineteenth-century man at his best. Putting on a silk tie or dressing in a tailored suit was more than a matter of pride or even habit. It was an act of reassurance, a confirmation that all was right with the world and that civilization was in command, for the chaos that was Reconstruction, the brutality he had seen and faced in Calvert and along the border had left their mark as surely as had his plantation upbringing. His courtesy, his genteel manner and strict ethics—they were his way of overcoming the savage that always lurked over the horizon or in the heart of every man.[13]

In the early 1900s automobiles began to appear in Fort Worth, and soon the Oxsheers owned three. One was a bright red open-air "Case." Trimmed in brass, it looked like a cross between a surrey and a fire engine. The Case had brass acetylene headlights, a hand crank, and "guaranteed" spring seat cushions—guaranteed for what the automobile dealer never made clear. When the salesman drove it to the house, family and neighbors crowded around in awe, touching the smooth, shiny frame, wondering what would be invented next. The second car was an Apperson "Jack Rabbit." Large and unwieldy, the Jack Rabbit drove "like a box car" and was never very practical on Fort Worth's narrow streets. F. G. literally put it out to pasture soon after he bought it; the Jack Rabbit became a work car on one of the

[12] Edwyna Thro, interview; Hodges, "Memoirs"; J. H. Bryant to F. G. Oxsheer, June 28, 1901, Oxsheer Family Papers.
[13] Hodges, "Memoirs."

ranches. More suitable to Fort Worth was F. G.'s battery-powered electric sedan. The special appeal of the "electric," as everyone called it, was its speed. The automobile could manage fifteen miles an hour on a straightaway—probably the reason F. G. bought it. In the electric he was notorious for weaving in and out of traffic, passing buggies and wagons, or racing men on horseback. If Mary was along she would tell him to slow down, but it did no good. He simply laughed in a teasing way, pulled down the brim of his Stetson, and whizzed off in a cloud of dust.[14]

The Oxsheers had plenty of opportunities to show off their automobiles; they were always on the go. Twice a year F. G. took the family to Neiman-Marcus in Dallas to buy their wardrobes for the seasons. Nothing was too good for his family. Mary had a wardrobe fit for the court of Saint James. Riding in his automobiles, they must have looked like a wagon train of the affluent. In Dallas they stuffed their cars with fur coats and stoles, hats, dresses, silk shirts and ties, waistcoats, boots, and an assortment of jewelry. Sometimes they took servants along to carry the load to the vehicles. In 1916 there was another special reason for going to Dallas. That year F. G. Oxsheer was honorary vice-president of the Texas State Fair. It was a proud moment in his life, though he would never have admitted it, to be publicly acknowledged as one of the greatest living cattlemen in the Southwest.[15]

Other times the Oxsheers left their automobiles at home and took the train to social events, business conventions, or on vacations. Every summer F. G. and Mary escaped the heat and spent several weeks in the Rocky Mountains of New Mexico and Colorado. Sometimes in the winter they traveled to California. Whenever he could, F. G. took Mary on his business trips. A cattleman's convention in El Paso meant hearing the latest reports on cattle exports, vaccination methods, or the beef trust. It was also a chance to meet with old friends such as Gov. Joseph Sayers or spend a day with Mary in the neighboring city of Juárez, shopping and taking in the bullfights. A Hereford cattle raisers' convention in Kansas City was an opportunity to get together with financiers and leading cattlemen from across the nation. It was a fast-

---

[14] Hodges, "Memoirs."
[15] W. A. Oxsheer, interview; Hodges, "Memoirs"; Cash receipts, Apr. 4, 1910, Neiman-Marcus Co., Dallas, Tex., Oxsheer Family Papers; Honorary vice-president's ticket, State Fair of Texas, 1916, Dallas, Tex., Oxsheer Family Papers.

paced life of elegance, wealth, and prestige that F. G. enjoyed, a world apart from those days when as a youth he first went up the trail to Abilene.[16]

One part of life that was not abandoned along with simpler times of the past was F. G.'s religious upbringing. He switched his religious affiliation from Methodist to Baptist—Mary Oxsheer saw to that—but his code of morality and notions of proper Christian conduct never changed. Firm and self-assured in his thinking, like most at the time he saw the world in neat, simplistic terms of good and evil, right and wrong. He wept unashamedly at Sunday sermons, prayed openly for forgiveness of sins, worried over the souls of the "unredeemed" in other lands, and set aside a tithe for his church and overseas missions. Card games were banned in his home. If one of his sons had lit up a cigar or cigarette in his presence, he would have slapped it from his mouth. In short, he was a Puritan in the twentieth century, yet even in religion he could find humor.[17]

F. G. and Mary were among the earliest members of the First Baptist Church in Fort Worth. F. G. was a deacon for years, but perhaps he was best remembered in church as the man who refused to serve in the "Preacher War." In the early 1900s the Reverend J. Frank Norris became pastor of the First Baptist Church, replacing the founding minister who had recently died. But he soon split the congregation into pro- and anti-Norris factions. Short-tempered, described by some as being narrow-minded as the pinstripes in his suits, he was a controversial figure from the beginning. Within the flock friendships dissolved and bitter words of recrimination replaced the Sermon on the Mount. Like a band of reincarnated Joshuas, the congregation marched into church every Sunday to battle for or against Reverend Norris. One morning a few of them nearly squared off with fists on the church steps.

F. G. was one of those who opposed Reverend Norris, but he had no intention of becoming an active participant in anything so inane. Instead, he called on Norris, hoping to clear the air with an honest discussion. As a man, F. G. explained to Norris, he had nothing to say

---

[16] Hodges, "Memoirs"; F. G. Oxsheer to Mary Oxsheer, Jan. 15, 1902, Oxsheer Family Papers; American Hereford Breeders Association, "A Hereford Matter," American Royal Cattle Show, 1901, Kansas City, Mo., Oxsheer Family Papers.

[17] Hodges, "Memoirs"; W. A. Oxsheer, interview.

against him, but as a minister for the First Baptist Church he found his credentials wanting. The talk was frank, but it solved nothing.[18]

A few days later the pugnacious Norris announced he was ordering the removal of the founding minister's remains from the churchyard gravesite to a cemetery. It had been a last wish of the beloved minister to be buried in the churchyard. That night as Norris sat in his office, someone fired a shot through the window, narrowly missing the "Herod of the First Baptist." The following morning the congregation was abuzz. Those who had opposed Norris feared for their lives and prepared for the worst. They quickly formed a vigilance committee and posted guards in front of homes. Solemn deacons and Sunday-school teachers nervously stood by their Bibles and guns.

In a day or two, several of the committeemen noticed that Brother Fount Oxsheer was missing. In fact, no one could remember having seen him recently. Panicked, the committee dashed off to the rescue, hoping they were not too late. They found F. G. at home, sitting on the front porch with one of his daughters. Wild-eyed committeemen quickly reminded him of the "danger." Did he not fear for himself and his family, they asked? In a fit of Christian regard they even offered to post a guard at his door if he didn't feel safe. With a smile and a twinkle in his eye, F. G. thanked the gentlemen for their concern, but assured them a guard would not be necessary. In his life, he explained with a smile, he had gained some experience in handling guns and men, and was confident he could protect himself and his family from Reverend Norris and his followers. The dispute with Norris raged on, but not for the Oxsheers. The family changed their membership to the Broadway Baptist Church.[19]

Fort Worth grew rapidly in the early 1900s, increasing from twenty-six thousand to a hundred thousand inhabitants in twenty years. Electric trolley cars and a bus service replaced mule power and carriages. On the north side the old saloons closed and the great Swift and Armour packing plants went up; on the southwestern edge of town Texas Christian University opened its doors following its move from Waco. Over the years the Oxsheers also changed. The children married and had little ones of their own. Mary put on weight and F. G.'s hair turned gray, then thinned. The family teased him about losing his hair, telling

[18] Hodges, "Memoirs."
[19] Hodges, "Memoirs"; Edwyna Thro, interview.

him that he wore it thin by combing and brushing every strand into place.[20]

Not every change was welcome or laughable. In 1905 F. G. lost his father, William Oxsheer. He died in his sleep, aged ninety, the man who had taught F. G. the importance of such words as honesty and self-reliance. In the early 1900s something else occurred; F. G. began to lose his hearing. Year by year it grew worse until he was nearly deaf. At first a doctor treated him periodically, "blowing out" his ears. For a few days he could hear as well as anyone, then his hearing faded again. This was an obvious disadvantage for anyone, but for a person who earned a living dealing with the public—buying and selling cattle—it was a critical handicap, and one of the reasons he sent F. G., Jr. to manage the Mexican ranch. It was difficult enough to understand English, much less Spanish. Somehow F. G. managed. He knew the cattle industry as well as anyone in Fort Worth, and his business associates were aware of it. They simply shouted when necessary and F. G. went on making money, far more money than most people with perfect hearing.[21]

The loss of hearing was an irritant to the family more than to anyone else. They went about the house shouting and screaming to make him understand. When hearing aids first appeared they rushed to buy one, but F. G. wouldn't wear it. The hearing phone that slipped into the pocket caused a wrinkle in his shirt, he said, and that would never do. So they continued their screaming until the 1920s, when the daughter of an old ranching friend sent him a hearing horn she had obtained in Germany. It was small enough to carry in his hand, and also made a dandy pointer. He took it with him on trips to his ranches and to the Metropolitan Hotel, so he could do business without being heard throughout the lobby.[22]

There was another invention F. G. didn't care for, probably because he couldn't hear—the radio. Folks never gathered to visit anymore, he complained, just sat around with necks craned like ganders toward a little black box, listening to some Eastern jack leg warbling about the plains or the "lone prairie." It was almost enough to make a man glad he was losing his hearing. If this kept on, soon humans would

---

[20] Hodges, "Memoirs."
[21] Hodges, "Memoirs"; Family Bible, Oxsheer Family Papers.
[22] Hodges, "Memoirs."

forget how to talk, wouldn't need tongues, or even minds for that matter—just ears.[23]

In Fort Worth F. G. always wore a Stetson, but black shoes instead of boots. His neat, close-cropped mustache and polished appearance gave him the look of a man from the East instead of someone from the range. Only the tanned, weatherworn face and calloused hands gave him away. His suits were lined with black taffeta; his spotless white shirts had pleated fronts and celluloid collars and cuffs. Every morning he dressed this way before coming down for breakfast. After eating, he thumbed through the paper, unaffected by the chatter of family and guests. In a few minutes he glanced at the clock or his pocket watch and announced it was time to go to work. Back up the stairs he went to brush his teeth and comb his hair. He was proud of those gleaming white teeth and he brushed them after every meal. Mary invariably fumed, urging him to hurry before he missed his streetcar, but he was not to be rushed. Not until he picked every piece of lint from his suit and combed every hair in place did he come back downstairs. Then, as if to make a mockery of his own fussy, meticulous manner, he sometimes danced a jig out of the house and down the front steps, with Mary pulling at his coattails, telling him to act his age. Somehow he always managed to be ready and waiting at the corner when the streetcar arrived.[24]

More than most men, F. G. was a bundle of contradictions. The same man who could square off against gunslingers and bandits and who had carved a cattle empire from an unyielding land might be seen in the early morning picking a bouquet of flowers for one of his daughters. The cattleman who was forever riding off from his wife for days at a time fretted over her smallest comfort when home. If he woke in the night and it was cold, he tiptoed to the front of the bed, rearranged the blankets and gently covered her. If Mary was sick, he waited on her personally, even though the house was full of servants. He was rigid yet compassionate, proud but humble, a tough frontiersman in one setting, a shrewd businessman in another.[25]

More than anything else, F. G. enjoyed showering affection and wealth on his children. When Mabel, his oldest daughter, married, her

[23] Hodges, "Memoirs"; Edwyna Thro, interview.
[24] Hodges, "Memoirs"; W. A. Oxsheer, interview.
[25] Hodges, "Memoirs."

wedding gift was a 28,000-acre ranch. When the second daughter Myrtle lost her husband to pneumonia and was left with two daughters of her own, he gave them his guest house. More important, he gave love and attention to his little granddaughters, laughing at their antics, getting down on hands and knees to share in their games. To have done anything less would have been unthinkable in his eyes. His youngest daughter Beal married a wealthy man, but she always knew that the surest way to acquire any luxury or frill was through her father. Birthdays, holidays, for any occasion or no occasion, he was forever buying something for his family. If he could have had his way, F. G. would have built another mansion three times the size of his own and housed the entire brood under a single roof. Yet for all the generosity and love, for all of the joy and laughter that filled his home, there was something terribly wrong in the family, something that grew worse every year.[26]

The problem was his sons. From the time they were born, F. G. dreamed of leaving them a vast ranching empire; but as the years passed, and as he tried to make places for them in his operations, they failed him miserably. All three of the boys acquired their father's tastes for fine clothes, cars, homes, and entertainment, but they learned little else, except to depend on him for everything. Only one, F. G., Jr., showed promise—none had the maturity of a twelve-year-old. The sums of money that all of them squandered, the costs of businesses their father placed them in that failed, were probably as great as the entire value of the Oxsheer ranches. If it were not for the grief they caused F. G. and Mary, their antics and business failures would have been laughable.

In the early 1900s F. G. gave Drennan the Pecos Ranch—nearly 70,000 acres—hoping it marked the beginning of another Oxsheer ranching saga. It didn't. Soon Drennan tired of the cattle business, sold the ranch back to his father, then packed his bags for college in Hanover, Indiana. The next three years he spent the proceeds on fraternity parties, high fashion, cars, and self-imposed vacations while his father paid for his tuition. Drennan never graduated; when he ran out of money he simply quit school. "I don't like to study," he wrote home, "and if you make me stay I won't do the work. It's cold in Hanover, and

[26] Edwyna Thro, interview; Hodges, "Memoirs"; W. A. Oxsheer, interview.

there's nothing to do." "Besides," he added mournfully, "the microscopes hurt my eyes."[27]

When he read the letter, F. G. probably recalled when he was a young man, and how he had planned to go to college until Civil War and Reconstruction put an end to those dreams. Didn't Drennan understand? The world was changing, and in the future a college degree could be priceless. Didn't he realize that everything the family owned had come from a lifetime of sacrifice and labor—from two lifetimes really? It began in the 1830s in Milam County when William Oxsheer built a plantation from a tangled river bottom. F. G. folded the letter, slipped it into his pocket, and said nothing.

Drennan didn't return home empty-handed. He brought back a beaming bride named Edna, like Drennan, eager to enjoy still more of the Oxsheer fortune—a perfect match. F. G. bought the young couple a furnished home and a chicken farm—something Drennan had wanted. But no sooner were they settled than the two were off on a honeymoon to Chicago. The chicken farm went broke within months. Next, F. G. bought them a meat market, but it also failed. In the end he sent the couple to "manage" one of his own ranches where, happily, others were on hand to do the work.[28]

If Drennan was laughable, Coke was hilarious. He also failed at a host of businesses: a meat market, a dry-goods outlet, an automobile dealership, and finally a lumberyard, all furnished, of course, by his father. Using his influence, F. G. next got him jobs at feed mills, banks, and stockyards, but in every case Coke quit or was fired. At last, hoping that his son might learn something of the cattle business, F. G. sent him to one of the ranches, but hopes were soon dashed. Every spring when the grass greened and the roundups began, Coke slipped away, following the New York Yankees around the country. Bags in one hand, father's checkbook in the other, Coke enjoyed the life of a European

---

[27] Edwyna Thro, interview; John Drennan Oxsheer to Frances Hodges, Oct. 24, 1964, Oxsheer Family Papers; Hodges, "Memoirs"; John Drennan Oxsheer to Mary Oxsheer, Mar. 4, 1907, Oxsheer Family Papers; John Drennan Oxsheer to Mary Oxsheer, Apr. 4, 1907, Oxsheer Family Papers.

[28] Hodges, "Memoirs"; John Drennan Oxsheer to Frances Hodges, Oct. 24, 1964, Oxsheer Family Papers; Edwyna Thro, interview; Oxsheer Brothers Meat Company, Business stationery, n.d., Fort Worth, Tex., Oxsheer Family Papers.

noble. He dined in the finest restaurants and lived in the best hotels. If he ran out of fresh shirts, he simply bought new ones and threw away his dirty laundry. His only communication with home in those weeks was through a string of canceled checks coming in from New York, Chicago, Detroit, or wherever the New York Yankees' schedule took him. F. G. would hire a private detective to find his son and bring him home, and for the rest of the year he lived in Fort Worth with his parents or at one of the ranches. But every spring, with the crack of the bat and the roar of the crowd, Coke disappeared.[29]

The greatest disappointment was F. G., Jr., the one who converted the Mexican ranch into a model investment. As the years passed, he slipped into alcoholism. F. G., Jr. was the key to the future. He was obviously the only son with the ability to manage the family empire of land and cattle, but how, if he couldn't manage his own life? When sober he performed brilliantly at any task; in some ways he was more capable than his father. But when he drank, F. G., Jr. became no better than Drennan or Coke. Twice his father bought him a string of businesses and ranches, but in each case everything was lost. For months or even years all would be fine, but then along would come a personal or financial crisis and F. G., Jr. turned again to the bottle.[30]

Many condemned the sons' behavior; it was easy to do. The pitiful old man, nearly deaf, working his life away while his sons indulged themselves at his expense: it was a touching image, but it was never that simple. The boys, like their father, were products of their circumstances. F. G. Oxsheer had carved an empire from a frontier that no longer existed. He made a fortune grazing longhorns on the open range and selling steers in a healthy market. The money he earned in this way became the foundation for nearly everything he achieved later. But by the time his sons were men, the open range was gone and the cattle industry was in a decline that would last for decades. In short, it was impossible for the boys to match their father's accomplishments in the cattle business.

The man who started with nothing but a few rangy longhorns and who built a fortune through grit and foresight—it was a glittering im-

---

[29] Oxsheer Brothers Meat Company, Business stationery, Oxsheer Family Papers; Journal of Accounts, Sept. 24, 1911, Oxsheer Family Papers; W. A. Oxsheer, interview; Billy Oxsheer, interview with the author, Fort Worth, Tex., June 22, 1983.

[30] W. A. Oxsheer, interview; Billy Oxsheer, interview.

age to hold up to the boys, but it was also unfair. The boys loved their father and wanted desperately to please him. They copied his manners and dress, but they could not duplicate what he had done. And so they sought escape from the relentless pressure. Drennan spent his time and money trying to convince himself and anyone who would listen that he was a "big shot" like his dad. Coke simply refused to grow up and face the challenge of his father's legacy. F. G., Jr. turned to alcohol. The night F. G., Jr. rode to meet Pancho Villa for the first time, he was already a desperate young man, searching for a way to work ranching miracles. He might have been great in finance, oil, or manufacturing. But he could not begin another ranching empire, not in the twentieth century; no one could.[31]

F. G. smiled and joked with his sons and always had a reassuring word for those in trouble no matter what their problems or who was to blame. If they wanted any luxury, it was theirs for the asking—he could never forget the poverty of Reconstruction and his helpless family in the 1860s. But the more he gave, the more dependent and insecure his sons became. It was a vicious circle. In the end, F. G. Oxsheer could no more keep from lavishing wealth on the boys than F. G., Jr. could turn down a drink.

The boys often bragged about how easy it was to get money from their father—"we shake the tree and the old man comes through." He bought them all Cadillacs, and if they grew tired of the make or color after a few months, they told him something was wrong with the cars and he replaced them. They could play him for a fool; they laughed; it was easy. They thought he didn't know what was happening, but they were wrong. Sometimes late at night, F. G. and Mary sat at the dining table weeping and wondering what had gone wrong, asking themselves what they could do to make things right. Invariably, F. G. tried to comfort Mary, assuring her that all would work out for the best, but he must have wondered how.[32]

In the early 1900s F. G. Oxsheer was easily one of the most successful cattlemen in Texas. Every year he paid interest on thousands of dollars in cattle loans as a normal course of business, bought cattle feed by the railroad carloads, and leased hundreds of thousands of acres. But his single greatest outlay of cash went to an account he labeled

[31] Hodges, "Memoirs"; W. A. Oxsheer, interview.
[32] Hodges, "Memoirs"; W. A. Oxsheer, interview; Edwyna Thro, interview.

"kids expenses." Somehow his boundless generosity had been warped and twisted into a vice. He could stand up against Klansmen, outlaws, blizzards, and drought, but he could not bear to deny his children. He worked on in his world of silence, indulging his family, remaining outwardly cheerful, and confiding in no one but Mary. If anyone asked about his sons, he always spoke with pride about whatever they were doing. But all the while he was hoping desperately that somehow they would change.[33]

[33] Financial memo, F. G. Oxsheer, Nov. 16, 1915, Fort Worth, Tex., Oxsheer Family Papers; Hodges, "Memoirs."

CHAPTER VII

The Gamble of a Lifetime

THE big windmill stood in the chilly gray dawn like a lonely giant, blades spinning in the breeze. It was twice the size of most and could be seen for miles across the open country. Beneath the windmill were several ponds or stock tanks, as they were called in West Texas, and around them were cattle drinking their fill in the early morning light. Some of the cows drank hurriedly then trotted off, returning to newborn calves hidden on the prairie. Others took their time to lick chunks of rock salt scattered on the ground before slowly walking away. The cattle were at the Doak Well on the Lazy Diamond Ranch.[1]

Watching the cattle, half-hidden in the faint morning light, was a man on horseback, the owner of all that was around him—in fact, the owner of most of the land and cattle within twenty miles. Dressed in a dark suit and Stetson hat, his lean frame straight in the saddle, he scanned the herd. In a way he was like the Doak windmill: a giant on the land. For thirty years, F. G. Oxsheer had reigned as one of the cattle kings of the Southwest. Even with the loss of ranches in Mexico and along the Rio Grande, he was one of the major cattlemen in Texas in 1917. There was still the horse ranch, the Z Bar L, and best of all, the Lazy Diamond, between Big Spring and Stanton. In Stanton even the little children knew of him. Whenever he arrived from Fort Worth and stepped from the train, he handed out silver dollars to the boys and girls. But that frosty morning, as he watched his cattle, he must have wondered how much longer it could last.[2]

The day of the cattle barons was at twilight. F. G. had known it

---

[1] W. A. Oxsheer, interview with the author, Fort Worth, Tex., July 6 and 7, 1983.
[2] Plat, Oxsheer Diamond Ranch, Howard, Martin, and Glasscock counties, Block no. 34, compiled by T. H. Seavy, June 28, 1913, in possession of Cy Marcus, Fort Worth, Tex.; Frances Hodges, "Memoirs"; W. A. Oxsheer, interview; Deed Records, vol. 67, p. 179, vol. 79, p. 122, Jones County Courthouse, Anson, Tex.

since he gave up ranching on the Staked Plains at the turn of the century. The cost of land, labor, equipment, marketing facilities, and borrowed money, all had mounted steadily for years—everything from freight rates on cattle to a sack of tenpenny nails. At the same time, ranch income was falling. Backed by science and modern management techniques, ranchers had become too productive for their own good. Every year they flooded the market with more and more cattle, driving down prices and consequently their own profits as well. The harder they worked and the more they sold, the worse their condition grew. By the turn of the century rising costs and declining profits were breaking up ranches as surely as nesters and barbed wire.

Now there was another immediate problem as well. The haunting specter of drought was again upon the land. It hadn't rained at the Diamond Ranch all winter. If rains didn't come in the spring, every rancher in West Texas would be desperate. Slowly he rode past the cattle, then pulled up and scanned the cloudless sky for a hopeful sign. At last he turned and loped off to start another day.[3]

It didn't rain that spring, and the heat came early. Three times F. G. watched dark, angry clouds sweep in from the northwest. The wind rose and lightning flashed; but then as if to mock him, the clouds blew away, raining all around the Diamond Ranch, leaving his own pastures to shrivel. The spring grass hardly grew at all that year. By May cattle were already eating the last of it down to the roots.[4]

All winter F. G. had fed his cattle on hay and cottonseed cake. Now, without grass, he would have to continue buying feed, at least until the rains came. He gathered every wagon he owned, bought or leased others, and hired extra men, then started a daily ritual of hauling feed from Stanton or Big Spring to the Diamond Ranch. They made two trips a day, sixteen hours or more on the road. There were thousands of cattle on the Diamond Ranch, and without hay and cottonseed cake they would starve. By midsummer the Diamond Ranch was cut off from Big Spring. The road had grown so sandy that loaded wagons couldn't pull through. The Stanton road was the only route still open. It became the lifeline of the ranch. As the drought spread F. G. was

---

[3] John Drennan Oxsheer to F. G. Oxsheer, Feb. 19, 1917, Oxsheer Family Papers, Fort Worth, Tex.

[4] John Drennan Oxsheer to Mary Oxsheer, May 3, 1917, Oxsheer Family Papers; John Drennan Oxsheer to F. G. Oxsheer, n.d., Diamond Ranch, Oxsheer Family Papers.

The Gamble of a Lifetime 99

forced to buy feed for the stock on his other ranches; his only other choice was to sell his herds.[5]

Just to make sure that he didn't run out of water, F. G. installed gasoline pumps at his wells. If the winds stopped for a few days and the stock tanks went dry, he would be ruined. Even with plenty of water there were problems. The cattle would stay away from the wells for a day or two, scavenging the parched land for grass. When they finally came in to drink, they gorged themselves, sometimes until their bellies popped. Many would drink their fill, then lie down in the water and mud so bloated they couldn't get up. If the men didn't get them to their feet they would ultimately roll over and die in a kind of waterlogged stupor. There was nothing to do but pull off coat and boots and wade out to the animals with a lariat. A man would loop a rope around the cow's horns, then tromp around its legs to free it from the mud. Once the animal could move, the cowboy staggered back to the bank holding the end of his lariat, mounted his horse, then pulled the animal to its feet and dry land.[6]

By July the temperature soared every day above 100 degrees; by mid-July it reached 110, then 112 degrees. Even in the shade the wind no longer gave comfort to man or beast. It felt as if "off a blast furnace." Rising with the temperature was the price of hay, wagons, and labor as ranchers everywhere scrambled to save their herds. Before August there was no hay for sale at any price. They turned next to buying shucks hauled in by rail from South Texas. F. G. had expected it; he had seen it all before when drought nearly destroyed the old Jumbo Cattle Company. To save time and cut the expense of rented wagons, he used the Jack Rabbit automobile to scatter shucks and cottonseed cake around the pastures. That way he could use the wagons strictly for trips to Stanton. He also began working into the night, driving the animals to water on horseback so they wouldn't stay out so long before they drank.[7]

Mary was in Fort Worth that summer, in poor health. F. G. wrote

[5] John Drennan Oxsheer to Mary Oxsheer, May 23, 1917, Oxsheer Family Papers; John Drennan Oxsheer to Mary Oxsheer, June 25, 1917, Oxsheer Family Papers; John Drennan Oxsheer to Mary Oxsheer, July 26, 1917, Oxsheer Family Papers.
[6] John Drennan Oxsheer to F. G. Oxsheer, June 27, 1917, Oxsheer Family Papers; John Drennan Oxsheer to Mary Oxsheer, July 13, 1917, Oxsheer Family Papers.
[7] John Drennan Oxsheer to F. G. Oxsheer, July 20, 1917, Oxsheer Family Papers; John Drennan Oxsheer to F. G. Oxsheer, July 21, 1917, Oxsheer Family Papers; Hodges,

her every evening or two and visited once or twice, but he didn't dare leave the ranch for any length of time. F. G., Jr. was holding up his end of things at the Z Bar L and the horse ranch, but on the Diamond there was no one he could leave in charge, except Drennan, and that was out of the question. No one knew where Coke was in these months, but that was probably for the best. Every morning F. G. was up before daylight and out with the men to feed cattle, pull steers from water tanks, or ride to Stanton to make sure his carloads of shucks and cottonseed cake arrived on time. It was exhausting work for a man of sixty-eight, but the fate of his herd was at stake, and he wasn't the type to stand around.[8]

In Stanton the cattle pens were jammed with cows, yearlings, calves, even bulls. Some ranchers were shipping their cattle to pastures in the mountains of New Mexico away from the drought. Most were simply culling their herds, cutting back to a fragment of what they had owned, hoping they could hold out with what was left until the rains came. But even as they tried to sell, it cost them. Every hour their cattle were in the pens waiting for the trains was another hour they were charged for feed and water to keep them alive. If the trains were late, they were forced to buy still more feed and water, or sell their cattle at a discount to brokers.[9]

By the end of summer there was still no rain, and a few men began to sell their ranches. No one had seen anything like it for thirty years. Men who had earned a living in cattle all their lives were at the end of their resources. Scorched pastures, once dependable wells that had gone dry, the loss of credit, and finally, the loss of hope; there came a breaking point. Old Man King, as he was called, a neighbor to the south of F. G., came to say good-bye before he left. He had been in the country for as long as anyone could remember, but was "gittin' out of this desert." He warned F. G. to do the same. "Ain't like it used to be, Fount. We're all fenced in now; free only as long as it rains and the

---

"Memoirs"; John Drennan Oxsheer to F. G. Oxsheer, July 27, 1917, Oxsheer Family Papers.

[8] F. G. Oxsheer to Mary Oxsheer, June 23, 1917, Oxsheer Family Papers; F. G. Oxsheer to Mary Oxsheer, Aug. 8, 1917, Oxsheer Family Papers; Edwyna Thro, interview with the author, Wichita Falls, Tex., May 30, 1983; W. A. Oxsheer, interview.

[9] John Drennan Oxsheer to F. G. Oxsheer, July 27, 1917, Oxsheer Family Papers.

banks give credit." There was silence for a moment. Then Old Man King stuck out his hand. Shaking hands he spoke once more before he left. "Git out man, 'fore it's too late."[10]

Maybe F. G. mulled it over, but not for long. If he quit ranching where would he go? What would he do? Buy a grocery store and sell crackers and prunes? Ranching was all that he knew and all that he cared to know. It was his chosen way of life. Maybe his sons would still find another livelihood. He hoped so. That was why he had wanted them in college and kept establishing them in different businesses. He knew the cattle business was changing, and not to the best interests of cattlemen. But he also believed that in 1917 he could still outlast any drought he faced. He kept on buying feed, and looking to the skies.

Normally a man could place an order for feed and pick it up in a day or two at the train depot. Loaded boxcars would be standing on sides, waiting. But by the end of summer this began to change. Something was standing in the way, tying up rail traffic all over the country—world war. The United States had declared war on Germany, joining in the greatest organized slaughter the world had yet seen. Everywhere locomotives shuttled boxcars of troops and supplies across the nation. Now ranchers were lucky if they could get feed within a week. In December, 1917, the government tried to smooth out the problems, turning over the railroads to a national war board designed to run the nation's trains from Washington. This made bad matters worse. Soon shipments of shucks and feed took two weeks to arrive, then three. In many cases F. G. bought carloads that were shipped to the wrong ranch; others were simply lost.[11]

None of this surprised F. G. Oxsheer. Once again the long arm of government had entered his world, just as in Reconstruction, threatening to destroy his way of life. Without feed delivered on time, his cattle would starve. Government, he said, had as much business with a railroad "as a hog with a sidesaddle." If politicians could find a way to make a bad situation worse, they would. Now he might have to cull his

[10] John Drennan Oxsheer to F. G. Oxsheer, June 21, 1917, Oxsheer Family Papers; Hodges, "Memoirs"; Edwyna Thro, interview; John Drennan Oxsheer to Mary Oxsheer, Sept. 21, 1917, Oxsheer Family Papers.

[11] John Drennan Oxsheer to F. G. Oxsheer, n.d., Oxsheer Family Papers; John Drennan Oxsheer to Mary Oxsheer, July 26, 1917, Oxsheer Family Papers.

herds like everyone else and sell some of his prize-winning stock—not because he couldn't afford them, not because there was no feed, but because Washington couldn't tell the difference between shipping his grain to the Diamond Ranch or Fargo, North Dakota.[12]

He was at Stanton one morning when a trainload of troops, dozens of them, maybe hundreds, stopped briefly. F. G. hadn't seen so many soldiers since the Yankees were in Cameron during the 1860s. They had been on the border, they bragged, protecting ranchers from Mexican bandits. Now they were on their way to save France from the Germans. F. G. said nothing, but he shook his head. When he owned nearly 100,000 acres along the border and was losing cattle and horses nearly every week to bandits, he had never seen one federal soldier. He sure felt sorry for the French.[13]

Eager to acquire beef for Allied armies, the government tried to rescue drought-stricken cattlemen in 1918 by freezing freight rates and, best of all, by offering ranchers low-interest federal loans. Everywhere grateful ranchers rushed to take advantage of the loans. But F. G. would have no part of it. Government gifts came with government strings attached, he said. Politicians would do as much good if they passed a bill outlawing droughts or dust storms. He also read that Washington would now force cattlemen who leased government land to stock a certain ratio of bulls to cows and only purebreds of a recognized breed. Wasn't that grand, he laughed? Government had finally discovered that purebreds produced a better quality of beef than longhorns, and that it took bulls as well as cows to produce calves. Hallelujah![14]

The boys didn't agree with F. G.'s attitudes. They thought him an old fool, though none of them dared say it to his face. He could get loans from the government at lower interest than from banks or friends like old man Slaughter, they argued. Didn't he realize how serious things had become? A few miles to the east, Drennan informed his dad, men were stealing what hay was left from one another's barns.[15]

F. G. told them that he might be old, even an old fool, but he

[12] Edwyna Thro, interview; W. A. Oxsheer, interview; Hodges, "Memoirs."
[13] John Drennan Oxsheer to Mary Oxsheer, Aug. 8, 1917, Oxsheer Family Papers; Edwyna Thro, interview.
[14] Edwyna Thro, interview; W. A. Oxsheer, interview.
[15] John Drennan Oxsheer to F. G. Oxsheer, June 12, 1917, Oxsheer Family Papers; Edwyna Thro, interview; Hodges, "Memoirs."

would not put himself in debt to the government, and anyone who tried to steal from him would get an old-timey lesson in what his generation did with thieves. He ordered double locks for the barn doors, then went to an old trunk and pulled out his long-barreled .45. And he never borrowed a dime from the government.[16]

Years before when he lived in Central Texas, F. G. occasionally dealt in cattle with a mysterious old Tonkawan everyone called Injun Jack. Solemn, sad-faced, Jack had been a figure of scorn to most. Yet the old Indian would have cut out his tongue before he told a lie or betrayed his ideas of right and wrong. He was a troubled old man who had lived long enough to see the end of nearly everything he cherished. F. G. thought he understood Jack a little better now, and he wished his spirit happiness and peace.[17]

It was a wild, confusing time for cattlemen, the worst drought in thirty years, driving many to the brink. At the same time, a government at war was scrambling for beef, pushing prices to the highest levels in history. For the first time in years a man could make big money in ranching, but only if he could survive the drought. F. G. could manage if the government would run the trains properly. He had spent a lifetime building a reputation as a man who paid his debts. His credit would outlast any drought. But there was another problem more serious than the drought and government combined—the continued soaring expense of his family.

Every year they spent more and more of his income until he could barely make enough to keep them in Cadillacs and high fashion, or pay for their entertainment and business failures. He was sixty-eight years old and wealthy. When beef prices fell after the war as they must, he would still possess enough to ensure a life of ease for himself and Mary. But he was not wealthy enough to indulge all of his family indefinitely. If something were not done, the boys would ultimately spend themselves into the poorhouse, and take Mary and him with them. He never considered cutting off the flow of cash. For F. G. Oxsheer there was only one solution—to earn more money.[18]

---

[16] John Drennan Oxsheer to F. G. Oxsheer, June 12, 1917, Oxsheer Family Papers; Edwyna Thro, interview; W. A. Oxsheer, interview.
[17] Marsh Mitchell to F. G. Oxsheer, April 26, 1898, Oxsheer Family Papers.
[18] Edwyna Thro, interview.

For months F. G. had mulled over the problem and the present conditions: the drought, soaring beef prices, his sons' extravagance and immaturity. What may have been the final incident that stirred him to action occurred in the spring of 1918 at the Diamond Ranch. All three of the boys were there for some reason, their Cadillacs lined up under a shed like shining, bloated hogs at a trough. Suddenly Coke decided to go for a drive, but instead of driving his own car he took F. G., Jr.'s. When he saw what was happening, F. G., Jr. raced out to stop him. Coke swerved to the right, just missing his brother, then tore through a barbed-wire fence, never slowing down. Within seconds the scratched-up Cadillac was leaving a trail of dust on the road to Stanton. F. G., Jr. ran back inside and called the law, reporting his car stolen. In two or three days a sheriff arrested Coke at a little town south of Waco. Coke assured them he was no car thief, that he had borrowed the automobile from his brother. "Just call the ranch," he told them. "They'll set you straight." But when the sheriff called the Diamond Ranch, F. G., Jr. answered the phone. "What's that?" he asked. "You caught the man with my car and he claims he's my brother? I don't have a brother; the man's a thief; lock him up."[19]

For the next few days Coke cooled his spurs in jail. No one in the family knew where to find him but F. G., Jr., and he wasn't talking. Mary was nearly frantic with worry. At last Coke persuaded the sheriff to call the ranch again and ask for his parents. This time when the phone rang, Mary answered. "Of course I have a son named Coke. No, he didn't steal a car; release him at once!" When F. G. heard the news, he was mending a fence line. He never said a word; he just kept working, thinking, and planning. It was time to act.[20]

While beef prices were still rising, F. G. planned to buy as many cattle as possible, fatten them in feedlots, then sell them in the soaring wartime market. No more hauling feed from Stanton or pulling cows from the mud—nothing but speculation in a booming market. If prices kept rising, he would be worth millions in a matter of months. He could retire as one of the wealthiest men in Texas, and one of the few who had made and kept a fortune in the beef cattle industry. No amount of family extravagance would be able to consume such wealth.

[19] W. A. Oxsheer, interview.
[20] W. A. Oxsheer, interview.

The Gamble of a Lifetime   105

The boys could buy everything from the New York Yankees to all the bourbon in Kentucky and still have money. Best of all, F. G. could ensure his ranching network as a legacy for his children and for generations to come. It was the gamble of a lifetime; he would have to borrow heavily and mortgage nearly everything he owned to buy so many cattle. If prices fell suddenly, he faced ruin, but this was not the first time he had taken chances. Beneath that reserved, dignified manner, there had always lurked the heart of a gambler. Just one more risk, one last throw of the dice, and the future was secure.[21]

Through the summer and fall of 1918 F. G. began buying feeder cattle, by the thousands at first, then by the tens of thousands. He borrowed every dollar he could from the private sector to buy as many head as possible, mortgaging his ranches, homes, cars, and home furnishings to raise the cash. When banks would loan no more he turned to friends. C. C. Slaughter loaned more than $250,000. Buying, feeding, and selling stock, then buying still more cattle with the proceeds, by November, 1918 F. G. Oxsheer possessed 185,000 head scattered in feedlots from Texas to the Midwest. He was one of the largest cattle proprietors in the United States, but he was also destined to become one of the most unfortunate.[22]

On November 11, 1918, the Great War came to a sudden end when Germany agreed to an armistice. A war-weary world rejoiced, but on the plains of West Texas F. G. Oxsheer's world was about to collapse. Within a few months beef prices sagged, then plunged downward.

F. G. immediately tried to sell his cattle, but it was too late. Everywhere frantic men sold their stock for whatever they could get, flooding the market with beef cattle and driving prices ever lower. In desperation, he asked his creditors for extensions on his loans. Some agreed, others refused, but it hardly mattered. Cattle prices fell so low, there was no hope of repaying his debts. In the middle of this calamity there was yet another blow; Colonel Slaughter died, the one man who might have helped him escape financial disaster. By the end of 1921 cattle prices were at their lowest level in twenty years. The

[21] W. A. Oxsheer, interview; Hodges, "Memoirs."
[22] Financial memo, June 23, 1918, Oxsheer Family Papers; W. A. Oxsheer, interview.

rains came again and the drought broke, but it no longer mattered. F. G. had gambled all and lost all.[23]

In the end, he sold his cattle for a fraction of what they had cost, then watched helplessly while nearly everything he owned was auctioned off to pay his debts. Nothing was left but his Fort Worth home, a few hundred cattle, and a remnant of the Diamond Ranch—10,000 acres—all that he had to show for fifty years in the cattle business, a life's labor wiped out in a matter of months. Once a cattle baron, he was now merely another small West Texas rancher. There was another disaster, too, and for F. G. Oxsheer something worse than the loss of everything he owned. In that same year he buried his youngest son. Coke died of tuberculosis, aged thirty-one and still a boy at heart.[24]

For the first time F. G. began to look like a feeble old man. His eyes grew sunken, his cheeks drawn. He had always been thin and wiry; now these characteristics made him look frail and haggard. He kept working and struggling, promising his family that all would turn out for the best, but he was no longer the man who had triumphed so many times in the past.[25]

After the death of Coke and the loss of his ranches, F. G. spent much of his time with Mary. She had been with him most of his life. It was almost impossible for either of them to imagine life without the other, and they grew even closer in this time of trouble and sorrow. They talked of the joys and heartaches they had shared, the children, and things great and small they had done together. Much of what they discussed was of the past, but they also talked of the future. Mary pleaded with F. G. to retire. They still had their home, she reminded him, and enough land and cattle to live comfortably. They could hire someone to manage the ranch, and in their own way still enjoy a rich and rewarding life. He was, after all, one of the most respected men in Fort Worth. He had done his best, she told him, and that was all any man could do. The time had come to enjoy the rest he'd earned.[26]

F. G. listened and nodded in agreement, the way he usually did when Mary talked earnestly. He knew she was concerned about him, but he paid no attention to her pleas. At a point in life a man sometimes

---

[23] W. A. Oxsheer, interview; Hodges, "Memoirs."
[24] W. A. Oxsheer, interview; Edwyna Thro, interview; Hodges, "Memoirs."
[25] Hodges, "Memoirs"; Edwyna Thro, interview.
[26] Edwyna Thro, interview; Hodges, "Memoirs."

stops working for himself; he goes on building and laboring, but for the sake of others. If a great national leader, he works for the sake of unborn generations; if a family man, for his loved ones. He scraps and claws, and sometimes works himself into exhaustion or the grave, sacrificing everything for a future he knows he will never enjoy. F. G. Oxsheer was such a man. In 1921 he started over, promising to build yet another ranching empire for his family. He was seventy-two years old and nearly deaf, but he was driven by a single-minded passion to regain everything that had been lost.[27]

[27] Edwyna Thro, interview.

CHAPTER VIII

Until the Last Dawn Breaks

HE stood on a grassy hill, head bowed, hat in hand. F. G. was home again, at the graves of his father, mother, and brother Willie. In the distance was Little River. He'd come back to Milam County to talk about a loan with friends and family; there were people who would help him get started again. But as he stood there—sunlight shining on his tanned and wrinkled features, his thinning gray hair—he was not thinking of money.[1]

He was troubled and confused, and hoped that somehow in this land of his earliest memories he would find answers to his questions and a way to make sense of a changing world. He still knew the cattle business, but the longer he lived, the less he understood people. What did they want, he wondered? What did they expect of life? There was greater material abundance and more technical marvels than ever before; he wondered what his father would have thought of an airplane. But at the same time there was more bitterness and complaining than he had ever seen. Men spoke of eight-hour work days as a goal or even a right. He had never worked an eight-hour day in his life. Others demanded job security, as if such a thing were obtainable or promised ultimate happiness. Didn't they understand that nothing was entirely secure? What would these types have thought of the ones who rested before him in their graves, when they were boarded up in a mud-chinked cabin fighting Comanches, and accepting it as a part of life? How could this younger generation have coped as he had in Civil War and Reconstruction, living every night behind bolted doors, ready to fight off renegades at any hour? The whole world seemed caught up in a strange mix of self-pity and anger, coupled with some kind of wild,

---

[1] Frances Hodges, "Memoirs," in possession of the W. A. Oxsheer family, Fort Worth, Tex.

materialist binge where people were determined to spend, drink, and play their way through life whatever the cost to themselves or anyone else. What had happened to ideas and habits like work, honor, and self-reliance?[2]

Worst of all was the way this new generation blamed its own personal shortcomings on someone else and turned increasingly to government as the solution to their problems. It hurt to admit it, but cattlemen had become some of the worst of the lot, calling for price supports, beef import quotas, and more federal loans; blaming their problems on meatpacking trusts, foreign competition, city folks, or anyone but themselves. Didn't they realize it was the same as signing away their birthright when they turned to Washington for help? If government guaranteed loans or price supports for cattlemen, then it could do so only by taking money from the pockets of someone else. And if government subsidized cattlemen in this way, then someday Washington would take from ranchers to pander to still another interest group squealing about their needs and rights. The only ones who gained in the end were the army of regulators, politicians, and paper shufflers who leeched a career out of making sure the whole giant fraud was kept in motion. If it were not stopped, the time would come when ranchers would be told how many cows to raise, where to pasture them, and where to market, in exchange for their subsidies. And someday maybe, everyone would be instructed where and how to live. It would all be done by self-appointed guardians of a nation's destiny and vote-stumping politicians, promising free gifts in the name of democracy and rights, but destroying real freedom in the process.[3]

At last F. G. raised his head. Birds were singing in the trees near the river, but he couldn't hear them. He put on his Stetson, then turned and slowly walked away. By nightfall he was on the train back to Fort Worth, with money enough to start again in the only way of life he knew.[4]

The 1920s were difficult years for cattlemen. Beef prices finally stabilized, but they remained low while credit grew tighter every year.

---

[2] W. A. Oxsheer, interview with the author, Fort Worth, Tex., July 6 and 7, 1983; Hodges, "Memoirs."

[3] Edwyna Thro, interview with the author, Wichita Falls, Tex., May 30, 1983; W. A. Oxsheer, interview.

[4] Hodges, "Memoirs."

The list of sold or failed ranches read like a catalogue of fallen empires in those years: South Matador and the Slaughter estate, to name but two. A few large ranchers held on to their land, thanks to the discovery of oil or to outside investments. But these lucky few kept their big spreads and cattle mostly out of sentiment or for tax write-offs. The old-style cowmen who earned their way by hard work and knowledge of the beef cattle industry were all but gone by the 1920s. Only a few survived. The sheer complexity of modern cattle raising promised to break up many ranches. Consumer tastes demanded a higher quality of beef that only grain-fed cattle could satisfy. Ranchers converted pastures into fields of corn and sorghum to feed their herds, but this meant purchasing expensive farm machinery, fertilizers, pesticides, and farm labor. It was the same problem that had dogged cattlemen for years—rising costs, dwindling profits. More than ever the cattle business was a gamble against lengthening odds.

If F. G. Oxsheer felt discouraged about the future or his chances of still succeeding in the cattle business, he kept it to himself. He plunged back into it like a man half his age, dealing in land and cattle as an independent broker. Nearly every day he was at the Metropolitan Hotel or the stockyards and Exchange Building, picking up bargains in cattle or land when he spotted them, selling for a profit whenever he could. Before long the "pitiful old man" with the hearing horn and the tailored suits was beating the odds. Once again he was making money in the cattle business. Soon he was also riding the train again, back and forth from Fort Worth to Stanton, to his favorite ranch—the Lazy Diamond.[5]

There was something special about the Diamond Ranch. The land was no different from other land F. G. had owned—the endless vistas, the fence lines fading into the distance. But in the great collapse, F. G. would have given up his home before this ranch. Maybe it was what the Diamond Ranch symbolized that made the difference—the culmination of a life's experience. Registered Hereford cattle grazed on most of the land, but now much of it was in corn and sorghum as well. When drought struck again, as someday it must, F. G. didn't plan to run out of feed or be at the mercy of government-run railroads. Hundreds of ad-

---

[5] W. A. Oxsheer, interview; Hodges, "Memoirs"; Edwyna Thro, interview.

ditional acres were in cotton. Twenty years before F. G. Oxsheer would have laughed at the idea of himself as a West Texas sodbuster, but not anymore. The years had taught him a grudging respect for plains farmers. In the last drought they had proved every bit as tough and dogged as cattlemen. Maybe they were right, and maybe he could also make a go of it. Besides, F. G. reminded himself, his father had been a farmer.[6]

He didn't plow with tractors, but with mules. They plowed furrows deeper and straighter, he said, and were more dependable. For years F. G. had raised mules as well as horses and cattle. His mule stock, in fact, was some of the finest in the state, having originated with the prize jack and jenny he had imported from Spain in the 1890s. Working the fields, plodding along behind the mule-driven plows, were Mexican laborers in white shirts and pants, and straw sombreros.[7]

At ranch headquarters two enormous windmills rose above the buildings and corrals, dominating the landscape. They were the kind used by railroads and could usually draw water even in the worst of droughts. A rutted dirt road divided the collection of buildings. On one side was a large barn with red paint peeling from the sides and a sheet-iron roof glistening in the sun. Connected to one side of the barn was a corral, and nearby, heaps of sorghum piled high to protect against rotting. Across the road was the ranch house—nothing fancy, just a frame box with an open-air porch resting on limestone. Old-style Texas cattlemen put up mansions in town for their families, but their ranch houses were usually crude and rustic, built for men who spent most of their time outdoors. The interior was plainly furnished. The only modern conveniences were electricity and a telephone. For some reason F. G. could understand voices over the telephone. There were no radios. Behind the dwelling were smaller houses for Mexican laborers, then fields of cotton and corn. A bunkhouse for the cowboys was a few hundred yards away from the other buildings. The pastures, like most in West Texas, were often sun parched, but with rain they turned into some of the finest grazing land anywhere.[8]

The cowhands who worked on the ranch were typical of the time. In winter they worked in overcoats and wore caps instead of Stetson

---

[6] Edwyna Thro, interview; Hodges, "Memoirs"; W. A. Oxsheer, interview.
[7] W. A. Oxsheer, interview; Hodges, "Memoirs."
[8] W. A. Oxsheer, interview; Edwyna Thro, interview; Hodges, "Memoirs."

hats. Some wore overalls and brogans instead of jeans and boots. In the summer they tied leather flaps across their faces like bandannas to protect against sunburn and sand. Many wore woolen shirts even in the summer, convinced that sweaty wool shirts kept them cooler in the arid climate.[9]

Like their boss, cowboys of the Diamond Ranch were living in a world of change. Many of the old chores remained: roundups and branding, pulling steers from water tanks, and riding fence line, but there were also new tasks. Cowboys in the 1920s vaccinated and dehorned cattle, worked dipping vats, and treated stock for screwworms or scabies. Just as in the old days, however, F. G. was always there, taking part in the work. When he came out to check on the roundups, he had a favorite bay stallion that he rode all day. Long-winded and more than fifteen hands high, the big horse had been specially trained for every aspect of range work. Sooner or later, at every roundup his men would call out to the boss, asking if he cared to change mounts; it became a standing joke. The answer was always the same, however. "No thank you, boys. I'm a little winded, but the horse is doing fine."[10]

Occasionally, F. G. drove around the ranch in the Jack Rabbit; other times he rode a horse or drove a buggy. The buggy was a good way to move among the cattle; they didn't shy away from it like they did from a man on horseback. Often he carried a notepad, checking off items as he finished a task or gave an order. There was a time when he had kept his affairs in his head, but increasingly he relied on written reminders. Funny, he thought, how a man's memory faded. He could recall details from fifty or sixty years ago, but might forget something from the day before.[11]

Perhaps he was not the man he had been, but he was still amazingly fit and sometimes even foolhardy. When he rode among his cattle in the buggy, F. G. carried a long black whip to break up fights between bulls. He raised only registered stock, and he couldn't afford to allow any to be injured. If two bulls fought he began circling the raging animals, cracking the whip above their heads to separate them, moving

---

[9] Edwyna Thro, interview; Hodges, "Memoirs"; W. A. Oxsheer, interview.

[10] W. A. Oxsheer, interview; Hiley Boyd, Jr., interview with the author, Lubbock, Tex., June 13, 1983.

[11] W. A. Oxsheer, interview; Hodges, "Memoirs."

in closer and closer. After the "battle" he sometimes bragged of how he had never lost a bull or a bullfight. Mary knew it would do no good to fuss about the danger of being a seventy-five-year-old matador, but she did a lot of headshaking.[12]

A continuous parade of visitors trooped in and out of the Diamond Ranch, just as at the home in Fort Worth. And of course, all were welcome. When visitors arrived F. G. took them about the ranch on horseback or in the car, showing off his blooded stock. He carried an old cow horn to call up the cattle for his guests. When he blew it, cows, bulls, and steers came trotting in from every direction, expecting to be fed. Nothing pleased him more than sitting amid a swirling mass of his cattle, proudly pointing out prize-winning animals.[13]

Every fall there was a party at the ranch. Half the population of Stanton was invited as well as every rancher and cowboy within fifty miles, and even farmers. Some of the cowhands didn't care a snap for those sons of "clodhoppers," but their daughters were certainly pretty. The old barn loft was covered in fresh hay, a band was hired, and tubs filled with ice and watermelons were hauled in for refreshment. It was a treat for everyone, and most of all perhaps, for F. G. In his day he had been quite a man on the dance floor. Once, he rode forty miles from his dugout at the old Jumbo Cattle Company to attend the Cattleman's Ball in Colorado City. He and Mary were a striking couple then. Now the two sat most of the evening, tapping toes to the music. All night it went on. Maybe once or twice F. G. and Mary would show the youngsters how folks danced in their day, and in the process, how a couple could still be in love after fifty years.[14]

Guests were welcome on the ranch, but even they had rules to observe. No one was allowed to ride F. G.'s personal saddle horse. F. G. was a pleasant man, generally quiet, but nothing could raise his ire like someone riding one of his cow ponies. It was an old Texas custom that a cowboy's string of horses was his private property as long as he remained on a ranch. Once a grandson made the mistake of saddling and riding one of these mounts. When F. G. discovered what had happened, he gave the poor boy a tongue-lashing he never forgot. In

---

[12] Hodges, "Memoirs."
[13] Hodges, "Memoirs."
[14] Hodges, "Memoirs"; Edwyna Thro, interview.

Texas, the old man explained, men had been shot for less. Only scalawags or renegades rode another man's horse without his permission.[15]

And grandsons were to leave the cats alone. There were twenty or more cats at the ranch to keep down the number of rats that pilfered the corn and sorghum. One grandson shot the tail off of a cat that had scratched him. F. G. laughed when it happened, amused at the sight of his bobtail cat. But to make his grandfather laugh even harder, the boy cut the tails off of six more cats one afternoon. When the old man rode in at the end of the day, he nearly "hit the roof."[16]

He was angry, but not for long. F. G.'s mind was on far more serious matters than unruly grandchildren or cats' tails. By the mid-1920s he was as busy as ever, improving the ranch, traveling to Kansas to purchase bulls or to Colorado to examine the latest irrigation techniques. Most of all, he was busy working with F. G., Jr., piecing together another network of ranches. In Hood County, southwest of Fort Worth, F. G. leased the Rock Barn Ranch and for the first time grazed Brahman cattle. All of his life he had been an innovator in the cattle business and age did not change him. He was convinced that Brahman cattle had a future in North Texas because of their ability to withstand heat and insects.[17]

He also leased the Johnny Washington Ranch in south central Oklahoma. This ranch was different from others F. G. had worked. The land was hilly instead of flat, covered with post oaks, and broken up with boulders, some as large as a house. Ranch headquarters was an enormous log cabin; the fences were split rails instead of barbed wire. In many ways the place resembled a ranch of the early 1800s. It had no windmills or improvements of any kind, just log structures, woods, and rocky hillsides. In the past the ranch had been worked by convict labor. The original owner, Johnny Washington, had known a governor who farmed out prison labor to friends and political cronies. By the time the Oxsheers arrived, the prisoners were gone, but there was someone else in their place. Living somewhere on the ranch was a character that the locals called "wild man." No one knew exactly where "wild man" lived in this rugged country, but then, no one wanted to know. In the

---

[15] W. A. Oxsheer, interview.
[16] W. A. Oxsheer, interview.
[17] W. A. Oxsheer, interview; F. G. Oxsheer, Personal Memo, July 21, 1924, Oxsheer Family Papers, Fort Worth, Tex.

past the few who tried to find his hideaway had been shot. He made his living as a moonshiner, selling bootleg whiskey to inhabitants in the nearby town of Davis. Anyone could leave money on a stump or rock near the edge of the ranch, come back the following day, and find a pint of whiskey. But those who tried to catch or track him took the chance of never coming back. F. G. and his cowhands certainly left him alone. Whenever they rode through the woods, they whistled, sang, and in general made plenty of noise to let him know that they were only after cattle.[18]

The Washington Ranch, the Rock Barn, and the Lazy Diamond—together they barely totaled forty thousand acres. There was a time when F. G. owned single pastures that were larger. The days of the big spreads were over, but in a way it no longer mattered. Instead of struggling with thousands of cattle on vast estates a man could do nearly as well raising only registered cattle, especially breeding bulls. For thirty years F. G. had raised registered descendants of the old grand champion Anxiety the Fourth. The quality of his stock was such that he could sell it coast to coast, sight unseen for the highest prices. In short, the Diamond Ranch became a breeding ground for some of the finest bulls on the continent. By the late 1920s F. G. Oxsheer was rebuilding what had been lost, just as he had vowed. In a time when cattlemen begged and howled for government credit or price supports, and every year more and more ranchers lost their land or simply quit, F. G. was prospering and expanding. He was the last of his kind.[19]

Maybe he was too old to manage another empire of ranches by himself, but if F. G., Jr. would keep working at his side, learning more and more of the operation, there was no limit to what they could accomplish. The two had known their share of ups and downs with each other. There had been tears, bitter words, and disappointments—but also laughter, tenderness, and forgiveness. They were opposites in so many ways, but they loved each other. To F. G. his son was never F. G., Jr.—he called him Buddie. All they needed was a few more years of stable beef prices—all they needed was a little time.[20]

They would never get that time. In the fall of 1929 prices on the New York Exchange collapsed, and the nation and world plunged into

---

[18] W. A. Oxsheer, interview.
[19] W. A. Oxsheer, interview.
[20] Hodges, "Memoirs"; W. A. Oxsheer, interview.

the worst economic depression in modern history. The price of beef cattle tumbled, and once again F. G. Oxsheer was backed against the wall. It was as if all of his hopes and plans had suddenly been snatched away just when they were within reach. Even the elements conspired against him; drought again spread across the plains. There was one temporary ray of hope in 1930 when oil companies drilled on the Diamond Ranch. Oil wells dotted the horizon to the south on lands that were once a part of the ranch. In the past F. G. would have scorned the idea of drilling rigs on his land—he felt they ruined the soil and made the cattle skittish. But economic disaster can change a man's attitudes, and he hoped they would strike oil. They found nothing. Adding to his worries was F. G., Jr.; once again, as in every previous crisis, his son turned to the bottle, becoming more a burden than a help. At last, F. G. sent him home to a doctor in Fort Worth. By the fall of 1930 his registered cattle were eating the last of stored grain, and he was running out of credit to buy more feed. He cut his herd to half their original number and sold the rest at a heavy loss. A few months later he sold still more. It was no way for an old cattleman to celebrate his eighty-first year of life.[21]

F. G. lost the Rock Barn and Johnny Washington ranches. He saved the Diamond only by mortgaging everything he owned. Even this, he knew, was no solution to his problems. Unless he could sell cattle at a reasonable price and repay his loans, all would soon be lost.[22]

None of the children realized how desperate it was; their father, as usual, kept it from them. That was his way. When they gathered at his table, they never imagined that even the silverware and plates had been mortgaged. Only Mary knew the real situation and what it was doing to her husband. For the first time in years she stopped buying new clothes. "What does an old woman need with new things?" she fussed. F. G. argued, but for once she wouldn't listen to him. "No, Fount. Put any money you make back into the ranch."[23]

Before the end of 1930 West Texas banks—those still in business—had stopped lending to ranchers. The government stepped in after the banks, arranging feed loans to cattlemen, but F. G. would

---

[21] Edwyna Thro, interview; W. A. Oxsheer, interview; Hodges, "Memoirs."

[22] Edwyna Thro, interview; Mary V. Oxsheer, Last Will and Testament, Oct. 26, 1932, Fort Worth, Tex., Oxsheer Family Papers.

[23] Edwyna Thro, interview; Hodges, "Memoirs."

have no part of it. He tried instead to arrange a character loan from large banks in Dallas, San Antonio, and Fort Worth. He quickly learned, however, this was pointless, dealing with fidgety loan officers in wire-rimmed glasses—the kind who lived or died with the price of gold, interest rates, and chalky medicine for their nervous stomachs. They would "bottom line" their grandmothers into oblivion before they would make a loan based on character to an eighty-one-year-old. What did it matter to them if an old man with a hearing horn needed money for his ranch? What did they care if he knew the ins and outs of the cattle business or had never gone back on his word or failed to honor a debt? What counted was assets against liabilities. This was the twentieth century; didn't the old goat realize a depression was on?[24]

Adding to his burdens was still another personal crisis. The family was eating breakfast at the Diamond Ranch when Drennan suddenly announced that he and Edna were taking a vacation. The two of them needed a rest, he said; "We're at the end of our rope." They were going to Mexico for a few months.[25]

At first F. G. thought he misunderstood. Not even Drennan would do such a thing. Every hand was needed if they were to pull through. But Drennan kept talking: "We wouldn't be in this fix if you'd take feed loans from the government. Listen to me, Papa; I've been to college; I know what I'm talking about. Everyone else is doing it so why don't . . ." He never finished the question. His father was glaring at him. It was a look Drennan had never seen. Slowly, F. G. rose from his chair, looking at his son all the while. His blue eyes flashed; his jaw tightened. For a moment F. G. was thirty years old again; he was in Calvert. Finally, he straightened himself and spoke in a low, steady tone: "There will be no truckling to the government in this household, so long as I draw breath." He said nothing more. Turning from the table he walked to the door, picked up his Stetson, and went out to his horse.[26]

Drennan stalked off in a huff to pack his bags, followed by Edna. By the time they left the ranch, F. G. was riding through his pastures, fighting back tears. He was losing his land, but worse, he was losing his

---

[24] Edwyna Thro, interview.
[25] Edwyna Thro, interview; Visas, John Drennan and Edna Oxsheer, Oct. 12, 1929, El Paso, Tex., Oxsheer Family Papers.
[26] Edwyna Thro, interview; Hodges, "Memoirs."

sons. Drennan and Edna never returned to the Diamond Ranch. They finally settled in California, but first they took their vacation.[27]

If only the weather and the economy would cooperate . . . but they grew worse instead. Never before, not in the 1880s, not in 1918, never had times been so terrible. By 1931 beef prices were at their lowest levels in memory, and the drought was converting West Texas into a desert. It was as if the "universe was cracking up." F. G.'s prized Herefords, now as gaunt and rangy as longhorns, nibbled at brittle grass, then began chewing at sagebrush. Soon dead cattle littered dry water tanks, and fields that had grown cotton and sorghum lay barren, feeding gigantic dust and sandstorms. The worst dust storms blotted out the sun, turning day into night, and piling sand against the ranch-house walls to the roof. Wind-blown pebbles struck the house like buckshot. A man could lose his way walking to the barn through the blinding dust. Sand blew into the home, covering furniture and bedding, coating everything in grit; nothing could keep it out. It got into the eyes, nose, and mouth, and became a part of life. Sometimes sand piled so deep in the attic it had to be shoveled out to prevent the ceiling from collapsing. Taking a biscuit from a plate left a clear imprint on the dusty platter; turning in at night meant shaking out dust-covered blankets and sheets. No one knew it at the time, but the worst drought in the history of the plains had begun, a drought that would spread from Texas to the Dakotas, leaving in its wake abandoned farms and ranches as well as shattered lives. Everywhere men and women prayed, children cried, but still there was no rain. Soon the merciless weather would cast pitiful thousands adrift, inspire John Steinbeck to write *The Grapes of Wrath*, and leave a bitter legacy called the "dust bowl" on the once fertile plains.[28]

On the Diamond Ranch F. G. threw himself into his work like a man possessed, driving his cattle from one fenced pasture to the next, hoping they could hold out on withered grass until the rains came and prices rose. Even in the worst of weather the old man worked, sitting astride his horse in the swirl of sand, his dark suit and hat nearly white with dust. He borrowed an old army flamethrower from a neighbor and began singeing thorns off of cactus to provide forage for his cattle.

[27] Edwyna Thro, interview.
[28] Edwyna Thro, interview; W. A. Oxsheer, interview; Hodges, "Memoirs"; Hiley Boyd, Jr., interview; John T. Schlebecker, *Cattle Raising on the Plains: 1900–1961* pp. 119–21.

Wherever he used the flamethrower, famished cattle gathered. When he stepped back, they would rush forward to eat the cactus, even while it was smoking. Every day F. G. was with the cattle and the few cowhands who still remained for mere board and keep, pointing orders with his hearing horn, sometimes getting down from his horse to help, then mounting and riding off to another part of the ranch to see what else could be done. Hard times and a savage climate—they were enemies he had fought all his life, and he had no intention of losing everything to them now. It was his own personal war. All that he had struggled against since he was a boy was embodied in this miserable drought and economic depression. From the Diamond Ranch there would be no retreat. Yet in the middle of this greatest battle, at his most desperate hour, came still another disaster, a calamity that finally tore his world apart.[29]

He was at the Doak Well with some of the men when he got the news. A hard-riding cowboy raced up, waving his hat and shouting: "Come quick, emergency in Fort Worth." F. G. climbed into the saddle and raced to headquarters and the phone. Something was dreadfully wrong, he knew. At the ranch house F. G. picked up the phone and called Fort Worth. What was the news, he asked? What was the emergency? He got his answer—F. G., Jr. was dying.[30]

It was impossible. It couldn't be. Alcohol might break a man's health, and take years from his life, but could it kill someone still in his forties? That something should happen to Buddie . . . it was unspeakable, unthinkable. Surely he would pull through—he had to. The drought and depression would pass. The two of them could still rebuild what had been lost. Together they could overcome anything. But without his son there was no longer hope. Without him nothing mattered anymore.

The old man took the first train from Stanton, agonizing every mile of the way, wondering if he would ever reach Fort Worth. He finally made it to his son's bedside in the early morning, but F. G., Jr. never opened his eyes. He died later that day, aged forty-eight, his father's last hope. It was February 21, 1931.[31]

After the funeral F. G. returned to the ranch, but not to work.

---

[29] Edwyna Thro, interview; W. A. Oxsheer, interview; Hodges, "Memoirs."

[30] W. A. Oxsheer, interview; Billy Oxsheer, interview with the author, Fort Worth, Tex., June 22, 1983.

[31] W. A. Oxsheer, interview; Edwyna Thro, interview; Family Bible, Oxsheer Family Papers.

Every morning he saddled his horse and rode out alone, returning at dark. No matter how cold or bitter the weather, he was gone all day, riding over the land he had worked and struggled to keep, asking the same question over and over: Why? Why had he been allowed to spend his life sweating and clawing, only to see his dreams destroyed? Why did Buddie have to die? The suffering, the heartache, the back-breaking labor, as well as the laughter and love—after eighty-one years it had come to this. It was enough to make a man raise his fists in screaming rage, or to fall to his knees and cry, hoping the prairies would swallow him before he opened his eyes.[32]

For a week it went on, the riding out at dawn and returning at dusk, the searching for answers to questions that no one can know. Unshaven, clothes wrinkled, he seemed like a different man. But somehow in those lonely hours another gnawing question pierced his sorrow and would not go away—the question of his family. What was to become of them? How would they manage in these troubled times? He was old and weary of life, broken in body and spirit, but Mary was also old and tired, and now a broken-hearted mother. How could she get along without him? What would become of his daughters, grandchildren, and now even great-grandchildren? More than ever they needed him, every one of them. He had always been their pillar of strength. How could he give up and turn away from them now? In the end, for F. G. Oxsheer there could be only one answer.[33]

And so, from the deepest corner of his soul the grizzled old cattleman made his last decision. He would go on. He would fight and struggle with every ounce of strength to provide for the family he loved. He would work until the last dawn broke on the final day of his life. The same impulse that had sent him up the cattle trails as a boy, caused him to put on a badge in Calvert, to suffer blizzards, heat, bandits, and financial disaster, again drove him on. Soon the spring roundup would begin—he would be there to take part. He would work like a man half his age if that was what it took to save his family from ruin. There would be those who would shake their heads, calling him a foolish old man, but let them. He would work until his loved ones were safe or until he dropped. He would never stop; he would never quit; he would never give up working for the family he cherished.

[32] Hodges, "Memoirs"; Edwyna Thro, interview.
[33] Hodges, "Memoirs"; Edwyna Thro, interview.

Epilogue

IT was early morning in Fort Worth; darkness still cloaked the city. Inside the train station there was no one but a man behind a ticket window and a few weary travelers, nodding and dozing in their seats. One of them was stretched out on a long wooden bench that lined the wall. The only noise was the distant, mournful sound of a locomotive's whistle. Outside, standing on the platform was a young woman waiting for the locomotive and for her grandfather, F. G. Oxsheer.

Standing in the dark, the young woman had been waiting for some time—waiting and worrying. In the last seven months she had watched her grandfather age ten years in appearance. She knew that he was desperately concerned for the family and his ranch, but her only concern was for him. Every day he was at the ranch in West Texas or in Fort Worth working at the stockyards or the Metropolitan Hotel. Sometimes he came in late at night so tired he couldn't eat. If he didn't let up, he would soon be dead. Worst of all, perhaps, was the way he tried to hide his anguish and exhaustion, always smiling, continually reassuring everyone that things were working out. He could fool some of the family, but not her. She knew him too well.[1]

She also knew that he blamed only himself for the loss of his ranches and the tragedies of his family, and that he felt he had failed them. She did not agree. In her eyes he was a great man: pioneer rancher, cattle baron, the man who would sacrifice everything, including his life, for the sake of his loved ones. Always he had been the tower of family strength and character, the one everyone turned to in times of trouble. But the young woman knew she couldn't change his thinking any more than she could persuade him to slow down and rest. In the end there was nothing to do but show her love, to be there waiting for him whenever he arrived on the train.

The sound of the locomotive's whistle drew nearer, then came the puffing of the engine, growing louder and louder, finally the rattle of cars and screeching of brakes as the train pulled into the

---

[1] Frances Hodges, "Memoirs," in possession of the W. A. Oxsheer family, Fort Worth, Tex.

station. Steam hissed and bells clanged as it finally crept to a halt. Porters in dark caps and white coats stepped from cars and began helping off passengers. Some passengers emerged holding sleeping children, others carried luggage. Within minutes the train was nearly empty. Finally the young woman spotted a familiar figure getting off one of the last cars. He stepped from the train, then carefully straightened his tie and the brim of his Stetson. Tall and lean, shoulders back, he was still a proud old man, nearly beaten down by life but still fighting.[2]

He saw his granddaughter and smiled. She walked up, kissed his cheek, and they went off arm in arm. They entered the station, passed the man still sleeping on the bench, walked across the lobby and out the door to a waiting taxicab. The old man opened the car door and his granddaughter stepped inside. But before getting in he turned and glanced up at the heavens to tell the time, just as he had on the cattle trails more than sixty years ago. The stars told him it was nearly three o'clock in the morning. Soon the sun would rise, shining across the city and the Texas plains, stirring everyone to life. Another day would begin, another day and another chance. He stepped inside, shut the door, and the taxi sped away into the early-morning darkness. It was September 25, 1931.

[2] Hodges, "Memoirs"; Edwyna Thro, interview with the author, Wichita Falls, Tex., May 30, 1983.

Postscript: September 28, 1931

Late Cattleman

F. G. Oxsheer, 81, pioneer Texas cattleman, who died Monday morning at his residence, 1119 Pennsylvania Avenue.

F.G. OXSHEER, 81 DIES OF ILLNESS

F. G. Oxsheer, 81, 1119 Pennsylvania Avenue, resident of Fort Worth for 36 years and pioneer West Texas cattleman, died at 2:10 o'clock Monday morning at his home after a short illness.

Funeral services will be held at 10 o'clock Tuesday morning at the residence. Dr. George W. Truett, Dallas, will officiate, assisted by Rev. W. R. White, pastor of the Broadway Baptist Church. Deacons of that church will be honorary pallbearers. Burial will be in East Oakwood Cemetery.

Mr. Oxsheer was born Nov. 9, 1849, in Milam County, near Cameron, moving to Fort Worth from Colorado, Texas, Feb. 5, 1895. He was the son of W. W. Oxsheer of Cameron, a Representative in the Legislature for many years. He owned his old ranch in Glasscock County at the time of his death.

Mr. Oxsheer was a deacon in the Broadway Baptist Church.

He was married May 28, 1873, to Miss Mary Beal, daughter of John and Mary Beal, pioneers in Milam County. Besides his wife he leaves three daughters, Mrs. Mabel Quinn of Big Spring, Mrs. Hugh Scarborough and Mrs. Ira McDonough, Fort Worth; a son, J. D. Oxsheer of Springer, N. M.; five grandchildren, Mrs. Luke Hodges of Wichita Falls, Mrs. Edwyna McConnell, W. T. Oxsheer and W. A. Oxsheer of Fort Worth and Lieut. John Quinn of the United States Navy; one great grandson, Oxsheer Hodges, Wichita Falls, and two sisters, Mrs. M. M. Letcher of Dallas and Mrs. H. F. Smith of Cameron.

124   *The Forgotten Cattle King*

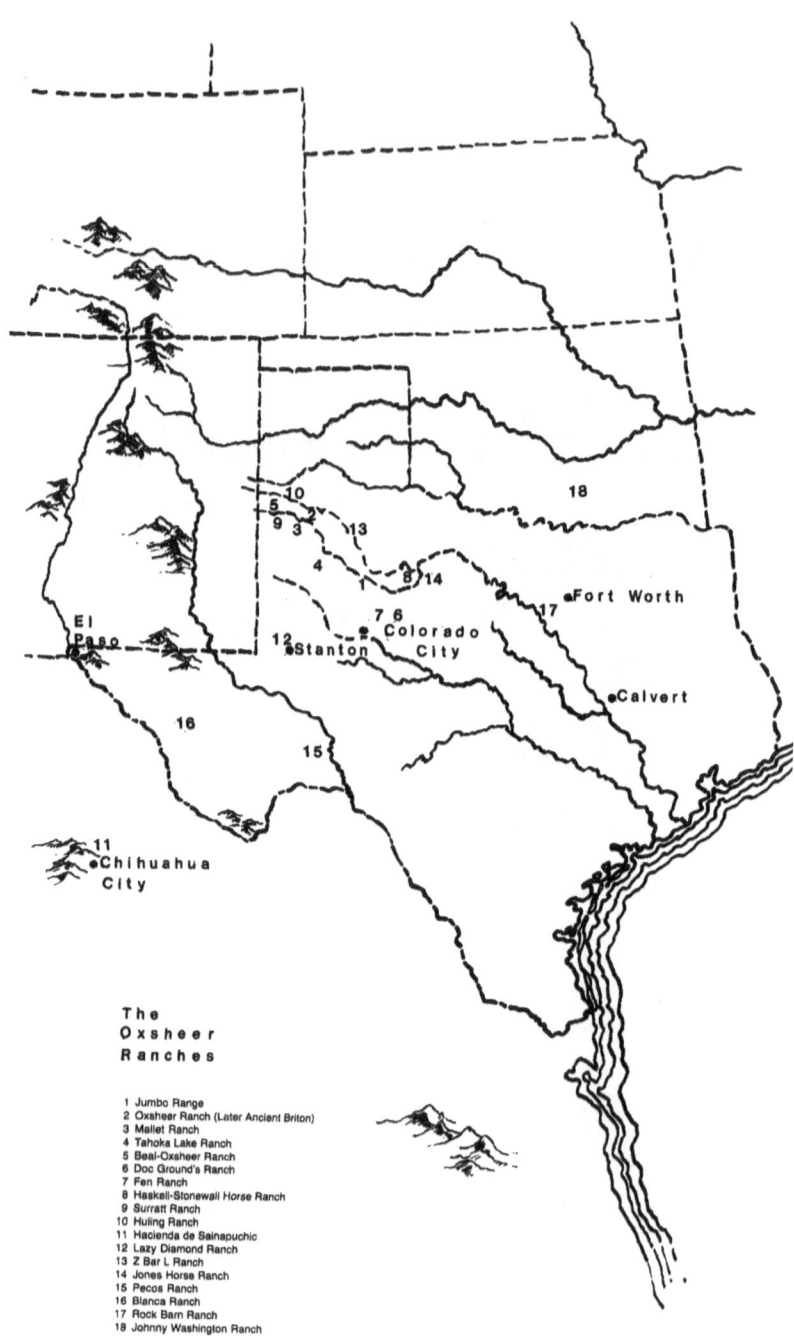

The
Oxsheer
Ranches

1 Jumbo Range
2 Oxsheer Ranch (Later Ancient Briton)
3 Mallet Ranch
4 Tahoka Lake Ranch
5 Beal-Oxsheer Ranch
6 Doc Ground's Ranch
7 Fen Ranch
8 Haskell-Stonewall Horse Ranch
9 Surratt Ranch
10 Huling Ranch
11 Hacienda de Sainapuchic
12 Lazy Diamond Ranch
13 Z Bar L Ranch
14 Jones Horse Ranch
15 Pecos Ranch
16 Blanca Ranch
17 Rock Barn Ranch
18 Johnny Washington Ranch

APPENDIX

F. G. Oxsheer Family

Fountain Goodlet Oxsheer
  b. November 9, 1849
  m. May 28, 1873
  d. September 28, 1931

Mary V. Beal Oxsheer
  b. January 8, 1854
  m. May 28, 1873
  d. January 16, 1937

Children
  Lena Mabel Oxsheer
    b. March 23, 1875
  William Oxsheer
    b. October 25, 1877
  Walter Lane Oxsheer
    b. October 9, 1878
  Myrtle George Oxsheer
    b. June 29, 1880
  F. G. Oxsheer, Jr.
    b. July 28, 1882
  Mary Beal Oxsheer
    b. October 24, 1884
  John Drennan Oxsheer
    b. December 4, 1887
  Richard Coke Oxsheer
    b. March 19, 1890

i

Selected Bibliography

NOTE ON SOURCES

Indispensable to researching the life of F. G. Oxsheer was a collection of family memorabilia I have entitled the Oxsheer Family Papers, held by the W. A. Oxsheer family of Fort Worth, Texas. The papers include a staggering amount and variety of material covering major portions of F. G. Oxsheer's business life. Boxes, folders, and file drawers are filled with letters, contracts, title deeds, tax returns, financial statements, canceled checks, bills, and bank notes. Many of the papers give precise and intimate knowledge of F. G. Oxsheer's ranch operations: journals, personal and financial memos, and cattle registers, to name but a few. Some of the most useful and fascinating information was a collection of business ledgers, inventories, and hand-drawn maps of the Mexican Hacienda de Sainapuchic. Much of the material also helped to confirm or supplement information from other sources. House plans of the Fort Worth mansion, business stationery, and numerous photographs all helped verify information from personal interviews.

As important as the Oxsheer Family Papers were Frances Hodges's "Memoirs," also in the possession of the W. A. Oxsheer family. Frances Hodges was one of the granddaughters who grew up in the home of F. G. Oxsheer. She had a sense of history and a deep appreciation for the historical importance of F. G. Oxsheer. The "Memoirs," above all else, brought the man to life.

UNPUBLISHED MATERIAL

Boyd, John Anna Dean. "Hiley and Margaret Boyd." Southwest Collection. Texas Tech University, Lubbock, Tex.
Business card. In possession of Cy Marcus, Fort Worth, Tex.
Coerver, Don. "Texas and the Mexican Revolution: A Case Study in Federal and State Border Policy." Texas Christian University, Fort Worth, Tex.
Hodges, Frances. "Memoirs." Fort Worth, Tex.
Murrah, David J. "A Cattle Kingdom on Texas' Last Frontier: C. C. Slaughter's Lazy S Ranch." Master's thesis, Texas Tech University, Lubbock, Tex., 1970.

Oxsheer Family Papers. In possession of the W. A. Oxsheer family. Fort Worth, Tex.

Seavy, T. H., comp. Plat. Oxsheer Diamond Ranch. In possession of Cy Marcus, Fort Worth, Tex.

INTERVIEWS

Bauer, Anella Slaughter. Dallas, Tex. Interview with author. December 15, 1983.

Beal, Robert. Fort Worth, Tex. Interview with author. June 30, 1983.

Boyd, Hiley, Jr. Godley, Tex. Interview with David B. Gracy, Jr. May 19, 1969. Oral History File. Southwest Collection. Texas Tech University. Lubbock, Tex.

Boyd, Hiley, Jr. Godley, Tex. Interview with David Murrah. June 2, 1970. Oral History File. Southwest Collection. Texas Tech University. Lubbock, Tex.

Boyd, Hiley, Jr. Lubbock, Tex. Interview with author. June 13, 1983.

Cooper, D. W. Fort Worth, Tex. Interview with author. September 21, 1983.

Jones, Mr. and Mrs. W. H. Fluvanna, Texas. Interview with Jeff Townsend. August 15, 1972. Oral History File. Southwest Collection. Texas Tech University. Lubbock, Tex.

Lyons, Cecil. Whiteface, Tex. Interview with author. August 20, 1984.

Miller, Mrs. Frank. Gail, Tex. Interview with author. October 11, 1983.

Oxsheer, Billy. Fort Worth, Tex. Interview with author. June 22, 1983.

Oxsheer, J. E. Fort Worth, Tex. Interview with author. August 9, 1983.

Oxsheer, W. A. Fort Worth, Tex. Interview with author. July 6 and 7, 1983.

Scroggie, Anne Beal. Fort Worth, Tex. Interview with author. July 19, 1983.

Thro, Edwyna. Wichita Falls, Tex. Interview with author. May 30, 1983.

Wilkinson, Mr. and Mrs. Sam. Stanton, Tex. Interview with Bobby Weaver. March 15, 1979. Oral History File. Southwest Collection. Texas Tech University. Lubbock, Tex.

GOVERNMENT DOCUMENTS

Borden County Courthouse. Deed Records. Gail, Tex.

Cochran County Courthouse. Deed Records. Morton, Tex.

Garza County Courthouse. Deed Records. Post, Tex.

Glasscock County Courthouse. Deed Records. Garden City, Tex.

Haskell County Courthouse. Deed Records. Haskell, Tex.

Hockley County Courthouse. Deed Records. Levelland, Tex.

Howard County Courthouse. Deed Records. Big Spring, Tex.

Hudspeth County Courthouse. Deed Records. Sierra Blanca, Tex.

Jones County Courthouse. Deed Records. Anson, Tex.

Kent County Courthouse. Deed Records. Jayton, Tex.

A Legislative Manual for the State of Texas. Austin: E. W. Swindells, 1879.

Lynn County Courthouse. Deed Records. Tahoka, Tex.

Martin County Courthouse. Deed Records. Stanton, Tex.

Mitchell County Courthouse. Deed Records. Colorado City, Tex.
Nolan County Courthouse. Deed Records. Sweetwater, Tex.
Pecos County Courthouse. Deed Records. Fort Stockton, Tex.
Robertson County Courthouse. Deed Records. Franklin, Tex.
Scurry County Courthouse. Deed Records. Snyder, Tex.
State of Tennessee Archives. Deed Records. Nashville, Tenn.
Stonewall County Courthouse. Deed Records. Aspermont, Tex.
Taylor County Courthouse. Deed Records. Abilene, Tex.
Terrell County Courthouse. Deed Records. Sanderson, Tex.
U.S. Congress. Senate. Committee on Foreign Relations. *Investigation of Mexican Affairs. Preliminary Report and Hearings on S. Doc. 285.* 86th Cong., 2nd sess., 1920.

NEWSPAPERS

Fort Worth Star-Telegram
The Cameron Weekly Herald (Cameron, Tex.)

BOOKS

Arbingast, Stanley A., Lorrin G. Kennamer, Robert H. Ryan, James R. Buchanan, William L. Hezlep, L. Tuffly Ellis, Terry G. Jordan, Charles T. Granger, Charles P. Zlatkovich. *Atlas of Texas*. Austin: University of Texas Press, 1976.
Atherton, Lewis. *The Cattle Kings*. Bloomington: Indiana University Press, 1961.
Batte, Lelia M. *History of Milam County, Texas*. San Antonio: Naylor, 1956.
Beezley, William H. *Insurgent Governor: Abraham González and the Mexican Revolution in Chihuahua*. Lincoln: University of Nebraska Press, 1963.
Brading, D. A. *Haciendas and Ranchos in the Mexican Bajío: León 1700–1860*. London: Cambridge University Press, 1978.
Brasher, Lillian. *Hockley County, 1921–1971: The First Fifty Years*. Canyon, Tex.: Staked Plains Press, n.d.
Cash, W. J. *The Mind of the South*. New York: Vintage Books, 1941.
Cattle Industry of Texas and Adjacent Territory. Saint Louis: Woodward and Tiernam Printing, 1895.
Clarke, Mary Whatley. *A Century of Cow Business: A History of the Texas and Southwestern Cattle Raisers Association*. Fort Worth: Texas and Southwestern Cattle Raisers Association, 1976.
Collinson, Frank. *Life in the Saddle*. Edited by Mary Whatley Clarke. Norman: University of Oklahoma Press, 1963.
Cook, James H. *Longhorn Cowboy*. New York: G. P. Putnam's Sons, 1942.
Dale, Edward Everett. *Cow County*. 3rd edition. Norman: University of Oklahoma Press, 1973.
De Shields, James T. *Border Wars of Texas*. Tioga, Tex.: Herald, 1912.

De Toll, R., ed. *International Directory of Pedigree Stock Breeders, 1930–1931*. London: Vernon Press, 1931.
Dobie, J. Frank. *A Vaquero of the Brush Country*. New York: Grosset & Dunlap, 1929.
Eggenhofer, Nick. *Wagons, Mules, and Men: How the Frontier Moved West*. New York: Hastings House, 1961.
Farrington, S. Kip, Jr. *Railroads at War*. New York: Coward-McCann, 1944.
Fehrenbach, T. R. *Fire and Blood: A History of Mexico*. New York: Macmillan, 1973.
———. *Lone Star: A History of Texas and the Texans*. New York: Macmillan, 1968.
Finerty, John F. *Reports Porfirian Mexico 1879*. Edited by Wilbert H. Timmons. El Paso: Texas Western Press, 1974.
Ford, Gus L., ed. *Texas Cattle Brands: A Catalogue of the Texas Centennial Exposition Exhibit 1936*. Dallas: Clyde C. Cockrell, 1936.
Gressley, Gene. *Bankers and Cattlemen*. New York: Alfred A. Knopf, 1966.
A Guide to the South Plains of Texas. Lubbock: Texas State Highway Department, 1935.
Guzmán, Martín Luis. *Memoirs of Pancho Villa*. Translated by Virginja B. Taylor. Austin: University of Texas Press, 1965.
Haley, J. Evetts. *George W. Littlefield, Texan*. Norman: University of Oklahoma Press, 1943.
———. *The XIT Ranch of Texas and the Early Days of the Llano Estacado*. 4th edition. Norman: University of Oklahoma Press, 1982.
Harris, Charles H., III. *A Mexican Family Empire: Latifundio of the Sánchez Navarros, 1765–1867*. Austin: University of Texas Press, 1975.
History of Texas Together with a Biographical History of Milam, Williamson, Bastrop, Travis, Lee, and Burleson Counties. Chicago: Lewis Publishing, 1893.
Knight, Oliver. *Fort Worth: Outpost on the Trinity*. Norman: University of Oklahoma Press, 1953.
Lewis, George M. *A Market Analysis of the Cattle Industry of Texas*. Austin: n.p., 1928.
Lister, Florence C., and Robert H. Lister. *Chihuahua: Storehouse of Storms*. Albuquerque: University of New Mexico Press, 1966.
Machado, Manuel A., Jr. *The North Mexican Cattle Industry, 1910–1975: Ideology, Conflict, and Change*. College Station: Texas A&M University Press, 1981.
McCallum, Henry D., and Frances T. McCallum. *The Wire That Fenced the West*. Norman: University of Oklahoma Press, 1970.
McCoy, Joseph G. *Historic Sketches of the Cattle Trade of the West and Southwest*. 2nd edition. Washington: Rare Book Shop, 1932.
Major, Nettie Leitch. *C. W. Post: The Hour and the Man*. Washington, D.C.: Press of Judd & Detweiler Inc., 1963.

Murrah, David J. *C. C. Slaughter: Rancher, Banker, Baptist*. Austin: University of Texas Press, 1981.
Nordyke, Lewis. *Great Roundup: The Story of Texas and Southwestern Cowmen*. New York: Morrow Publishing, 1955.
Parker, Richard Denny. *Historical Recollections of Robertson County Texas with Biographical and Genealogical Notes on the Pioneers and Their Families*. Edited by Nona Clement Parker. Salado, Tex.: Anson Jones Press, 1955.
Pelzer, Louis. *The Cattleman's Frontier*. Glendale, Calif.: Arthur H. Clark, 1936.
Reynolds, Robert. *Texas*. Portland: Charles H. Belding, 1973.
Schlebecker, John T. *Cattle Raising on the Plains: 1900–1961*. Lincoln: University of Nebraska Press, 1963.
Skaggs, Jimmy. *The Cattle Trailing Industry: Between Supply and Demand, 1866–1890*. Lawrence: University of Kansas Press, 1973.
Smithers, W. D. *Early Trail Drives in the Big Bend*. El Paso: Texas Western Press, 1979.
Tannenbaum, Frank. *The Mexican Agrarian Revolution*. Washington, D.C.: Brookings Institution, 1930.
Texas Almanac and State Industrial Guide, 1974–1975. Dallas: A. H. Belo, 1973.
Webb, Walter Prescott. *The Great Plains*. New York: Grosset & Dunlap, 1931.
―――. *The Texas Rangers: A Century of Frontier Defense*. Boston: Houghton Mifflin, 1935.
―――, editor in chief. *The Handbook of Texas*. Austin: Texas State Historical Association, 1952.
Whitlock, V. H. *Cowboy Life on the Llano Estacado*. Norman: University of Oklahoma Press, 1970.
Wilcox, Earley Vernon, and Clarence Beaman Smith. *Farmers Encyclopedia of Agriculture*. New York: Orange Judd, 1914.
Williams, J. W. *Old Texas Trails*. Edited by Kenneth F. Neighbors. Burnet, Tex.: Eakin Press, 1979.
Worcester, Don. *The Chisholm Trail: High Road of the Cattle Kingdom*. Lincoln: University of Nebraska Press, 1980.

ARTICLES

Aten, Ira. "Crossing High Water in a Wagon." *Frontier Times* 18, no. 8 (May, 1941): 367–68.
Biggers, Don H. "From Cattle Range to Cotton Patch." *Frontier Times* 21, no. 4 (January, 1944): 153–68; (February, 1944): 199–214.
Brand, Donald D. "The Early History of the Range Cattle Industry in Northern Mexico." *Agricultural History* 35 (July, 1961): 132–39.
Burke, J. F. "Jim Roberts—Old Hand with a Gun." *Frontier Times* 54 (July, 1980): 12–15.

Clarke, Mary Whatley. "Big Drouth of 1886." *The Cattleman* 30 (January, 1944): 16–18.

———. "The World's Greatest Cattle King." *The Cattleman* 43 (August, 1956): 58–68.

Coleman, Max. "Frontier Sheriffs Played Important Role." *Frontier Times* 13, no. 2 (November, 1935): 95–100.

Dennis, Dorothy Austin. "Major Willa Viley Johnson and the Kentucky and Magnolia Cattle Companies." *West Texas Historical Association Year Book* 48 (1972): 135–53.

Dolman, Wilson E., III. "Conflicts over Land: The Settler and the Rancher in West Texas." *West Texas Historical Association Year Book* 50 (1974): 61–75.

Gill, Larry. "From Butcher Boy to Beef King: The Gold Camp Days of Conrad Kohrs." *Montana* 8, no. 2 (Spring, 1958): 40–55.

Griffin, Guy J. "De-Gunning the Gun-Men." *Frontier Times* 15, no. 4, (September, 1938): 563–68.

Hendrix, John M. "Tribute Paid to Negro Cowmen." *The Cattleman* 22 (February, 1936): 24–26.

Holden, W. C. "The Problem of Maintaining the Solid Range in the Spur Ranch." *Southwestern Historical Quarterly* 34, no. 1, (July, 1930): 1–19.

Holt, R. D. "Cattlemen and Settlers 'Rushed' for School Lands." *The Cattleman* 21 (August, 1934): 20–24.

Jones, Mrs. J. Lee, and O. W. Clive. "Frontier Days in Mitchell County and Colorado City, 1876–1885." *West Texas Historical Association Year Book* 16 (October, 1940): 28–60.

Jones, Mrs. J. Lee, and Rupert N. Richardson. "Colorado City, the Cattleman's Capital." *West Texas Historical Association Year Book* 19 (October, 1943): 36–63.

Jordan, Terry G. "Windmills in Texas." *Agricultural History* 37 (April, 1963): 80–85.

Katz, Friedrich. "Labor Conditions in Haciendas in Porfirian Mexico: Some Trends and Tendencies." *The Hispanic American Historical Review* 54 (February, 1974): 1–47.

Kemp, L. W., ed. "Early Days in Milam County: Reminiscences of Susan Turnham McCown." *Southwestern Historical Quarterly* 53 (January, 1947): 367–76.

Loughead, Flora Haines. "Those Old California Vaqueros." *Frontier Times* 52 (August-September, 1978): 28–29, 62.

Miller, Edna Clark. "Jumbo Ranch." *Borden Citizen* 4 (June, 1969): 1–6.

Mörner, Magnus. "The Spanish American Hacienda: A Survey of Recent Research and Debate." *The Hispanic American Historical Review* 53 (May, 1973): 183–216.

Moses, Tad. "Early Day Cattlemen." *The Cattleman* 34 (December, 1947): 72–73.

Murchinson, Ivan. As told to K. F. Neighbors. "Ranching on the Pecos at the Turn of the Twentieth Century." *West Texas Historical Association Year Book* 53 (1977): 127–36.
Murrah, David J., and Elvis E. Fleming. "C. C. Slaughter's Sir Bedwell." *The Cattleman* 60 (August, 1973): 66–75.
Murray, Myrtle. "Home Life on Early Ranches of Southwest Texas." *The Cattleman* 27 (October, 1940): 53–58.
Nelson, Bascom. "The Ways of a Vaquero." *The Cattleman* 54 (May, 1968): 46–47.
Nolen, O. W. "Sheriff When Nueces Was Dead Line." *Frontier Times* 9, no. 4 (January, 1932): 165–68.
Remington, Frederic. Submitted by Louis William Steinwedel. "In the Sierra Madre with the Punchers." *Frontier Times* 38 (December-January, 1964): 16–17, 54–56.
Utley, Robert M. "The Range Cattle Industry in the Big Bend." *Southwestern Historical Quarterly* 69 (April, 1966): 419–41.
Watkins, Orville R. "Hockley County: From Cattle Ranchers to Farms." *West Texas Historical Association Year Book* 17 (October, 1941): 44–70.
"What the Cattlemen Are Doing." *The Cattleman* 3 (January, 1917): 33.
Wilmeth, A. C. "The Story of Block No. 97." *West Texas Historical Association Year Book* 5 (June, 1929): 125–27.

Index

Abilene, Kansas, 10, 11, 12, 16, 17, 88
Ancient Briton, 61
Ancient Briton Ranch, 61, 64–65, 67
Anxiety the Fourth, 61, 115
Arango, Doroteo, 73. *See also* Pancho Villa
automobiles, 86, 87

Babricora, 72
barbed wire, 22, 59, 60–61, 65, 71, 98
Beal, A. A. "Turk," 38, 44, 66
Beal, H. C. "Gulf," 38, 44
Beal, John, 12, 13, 16, 18, 19, 30, 37, 44, 55
Beal, "Massa John," 9–10, 12
Beal, Nick, 12, 18, 19, 30, 37, 38, 44, 55
Beal, Richard, 37–38
Beal family, 9, 12, 13, 16, 18, 19, 40, 55
beef bonanza, 30, 49
Big Spring, Texas, 82, 97, 98
Blanca Ranch, 74, 75, 79
blizzards, 42–44, 53, 56
bootlegger, 114–15
Borden County, 66
Boyd, Hiley, 57–58, 68
Brahman cattle, 114
Broadway Baptist Church, 89
bronc busting, 58–59
Buckle or Buckle B brand, 41, 48, 55
Buddie, 115, 119, 120. *See also* Oxsheer, F. G., Jr.
Bull Run trail, 44–47

California, 87, 118
Calvert, Texas, 23–29, 86
Cameron, Texas, 7, 9, 15, 102
Cap Rock, 36–37, 40, 49, 50, 53, 55

Carter, Amon, 85
cattle industry: changing conditions in, 44, 48–49, 56, 59, 60–62, 65–67; decline of, 97–98, 100–101, 105, 109–10; emergence of, 10, 22, 23, 30, 34, 39–40
Central Texas, 9, 12, 37, 38, 60, 103
Chihuahua, Mexico, 68–70, 76, 82. *See also* Mexico *and* Mexican Revolution
Chisholm Trail, 10, 12–13, 15–17
Colorado, 87, 114
Colorado City, Texas, 30, 33, 34–35, 36, 48, 61, 81, 113
Colorado River, 31
Colt "Peacemaker" or long-barreled .45, 26, 29, 103
Comanches, 37, 40, 44, 50, 52, 74, 108
Concho River, 45, 47, 48
Cooper, Gary, 85
cotton, 10, 18, 111
Cousin Jennie, 85
cowboys, 60; backgrounds, 11; character, 39, 56–57; clothing, 111–12; daily life, 41; leisure time, 16, 17, 113. *See also* Boyd, Hiley; Slick; *and* vaqueros
Cowtown, 81. *See also* Fort Worth, Texas
Crosby County, 74
Cuchillo Parado, 76

Dallas, Texas, 61, 87, 117
Davis, J. T., 37
Davis, Oklahoma, 115
Devil's River, 44
Diamond Ranch (Lazy Diamond), 4, 74, 97, 98–106, 110–11, 113–14, 116–19
Díaz, Porfirio, 69, 76
Doak Well, 97, 119

Doc Grounds Ranch, 56
Double Mountain Fork of the Brazos, 36, 44, 48
drag riders, 12
Drennan, John, 27, 28, 37, 55
droughts, 48–49, 53–54, 56, 98–106, 116–19
dugout, 41–42
Durham cattle, 60, 61
dust bowl, 118

economic depressions, 4, 49, 54, 56, 105–106, 115–19
Emma (former slave), 7, 10
Exchange Building, 81, 110

farmers or nesters, 65–67, 98, 111, 113
Fen Ranch, 56
First Baptist Church, 88–89
flank riders, 12
Fort Worth, Texas, 12, 80–90, 97, 106, 109, 110, 116, 117, 119, 121
Franklin, Texas, 29

Gail, Texas, 66
Gates, John, 22
Glasscock County, 74
González, Abraham, 72–73, 76
Goodnight, Charles, 30, 60–61
Gould, E. W., Jr., 70, 73
gunmen, 27–28

hacendado, 69, 73
Hanover College, 92
Harris, A. J., 55
Haskell County, 56
Hearst, George, 72
Herefords, 4, 59, 60–62, 71, 87, 110, 112, 113, 115, 118
Holly brothers, 76
Holsteins, 71
Hood County, 114
horse ranch, 56, 97
Howard County, 74
Huling, M. B., 55
Huling Ranch, 56
Huntsville, Texas, 28, 29

Indians, 30, 39–41, 52
Indian Territory, 12, 15, 56
Injun Jack, 103

Jack Rabbit automobile, 86, 99, 112
Jake's Restaurant, 35
Johnny Washington Ranch, 114–15, 116
Jones County Horse Ranch, 114–15, 116
Jumbo Cattle Company, 30, 36–41, 42–49, 66–67, 99, 113

Kansas, 12, 16, 19, 61, 114
Kate (servant), 22, 36, 85–86
Ku Klux Klan, 85–86

Lampasas, Texas, 29, 30
land laws, 65–67
la tienda de raya, 69
law enforcement, 25–29
Lazy Diamond brand, 55
Lazy S Ranch, 67, 68
Little River, 7, 10, 15, 20, 69, 108
Llano Estacado, 36–37, 42–44, 48–50, 53–56, 59–62, 65–68
longhorns, 9, 16, 37, 43–47, 48, 59, 94
Long S Ranch, 37, 60
Low Plains, 56

McCoy, Joseph, 10
Mallet Ranch, 55
Martin County, 74
Metropolitan Hotel, 81–82, 90, 110, 121
Mexican hacienda, 69–71. *See also* Sainapuchic
Mexican Hereford Breeding and Importing Company, 71
Mexican laborers, 69, 70–71, 72, 111
Mexican Revolution, 75–76, 77–79, 86, 102
Mexico, 50, 68–71, 72, 73, 74, 75–79, 102
Milam County, 9, 10, 13, 14, 26, 40, 82, 93, 108
Miles (former slave), 7, 10
Muchakooago Peak, 36
mules, 4, 11

Neil, Sam, 77–78
Neiman-Marcus, 87
New Mexico, 50, 52, 55, 87, 100
Nolan County, 56
North Plains, 49
North Texas, 56, 114
Norris, J. Frank, 88–89
Noss (servant), 22–23, 36

Index

oil, 110, 116
Oklahoma, 114
Old Man King, 100–101
open range, 30, 39–40, 59–60, 65–67, 94
Oxsheer, Beal (daughter), 21, 63, 82, 92
Oxsheer, Coke (son), 21, 63, 82, 93–94, 95, 100, 103, 104, 106
Oxsheer, Drennan (son), 21, 55, 63, 82, 92–93, 94, 95, 100, 102, 103, 117–18
Oxsheer, Edna (daughter-in-law), 93, 117–18
Oxsheer, F. G., Jr. (son): birth, 20; character, 90, 92, 94–95, 116; death, 119; family fight, 104; managing ranches, 63, 71–73, 90, 100, 114, 115; and Pancho Villa, 73
Oxsheer, Mabel (daughter), 20, 22–23, 29, 31, 62–63, 82, 91–92
Oxsheer, Martha (mother), 7, 56, 63
Oxsheer, Mary Beal (wife): appearance, 19, 89; daily life, 21, 36, 48, 82; and family, 95, 104, 106, 116, 120; health, 99–100; leisure time, 87, 113; marriage, 19; religion, 88; and servants, 22, 82, 84
Oxsheer, Myrtle (daughter), 20, 31, 82, 92
Oxsheer, Walter (son), 20
Oxsheer, William (father), 7, 10–11, 15, 19, 25–26, 31, 40–41, 55, 90, 93
Oxsheer, Willie (brother), 15, 20
Oxsheer, Willie (son), 20
Oxsheer mansion, 83–85

Pancho Villa, 73, 76, 76 n.23, 95
Pecos Ranch, 74, 75, 79, 92
Pecos River, 44, 45, 50
peon, 69, 70, 71, 72, 73, 75
point riders, 12
Post, C. W., 67
prairie fire, 64–65
"Preacher War," 88–89
prison wagon, 28–29

radio, 90–91, 111
railroads, 3–5, 10, 23, 34, 65, 80–81, 82, 99, 100, 101–103, 110, 121–22
Reconstruction, 6, 7, 9–10, 19, 61, 86, 95, 101, 108
remuda, 18
renegades, 7, 9, 10–11
Republic of Texas, 50

Richardson, Sid, 85
riding line, 41
Rio Grande, 44, 77, 78
road branding, 71
Robertson County, 23
Rock Barn Ranch, 114, 115, 116
Rockefeller, Frank, 4, 71
rurales, 76

Sainapuchic, 70–72, 73, 75, 76, 90
San Andrés, 76
Sanderson, Texas, 75
Sayers, Gov. Joseph, 87
servants, 7, 10, 13, 22–23, 31, 35–36, 69, 71, 82, 84, 85, 87, 91
Sierra Blanca, Texas, 75
Sierra Madre, 70, 73
Slaughter, C. C., 4, 30, 37, 60–62, 67–68, 80, 102, 105
slaves or slavery, 7, 10, 13, 15, 22, 85
Slick (black cowboy), 58–59
South Matador Ranch, 110
South Texas, 77, 99
Spanish conquistadores, 50, 52
Spanish dagger, 74–75
Staked Plains, 36–37, 42–44, 48–49, 50, 52, 53–55, 61, 67–68, 98
Stanton, Texas, 3, 4, 82, 97, 98, 99, 100, 102, 104, 110, 113, 119
stock tanks, 97, 99
stockyards, 81, 110, 121
Stonewall County, 56
Surratt Ranch, 56, 58
Swan Cattle Company, 49, 61
Sweetwater, Texas, 56, 85
swing riders, 12

Tahoka Lake Ranch, 55
Taylor County, 56
Texas Christian University, 89
Texas fever, 16
Texas Rangers, 29, 77, 78–79
Texas South Plains, 4
Texas State Fair, 4, 87
Texas Street, 17. *See also* Abilene, Kansas
tienda de raya, 69
top hands, 11
trail boss, 11
Trans-Pecos region, 74–75, 79
Trinity River, 81

United States government, 52, 101–105, 116–17

vaqueros, 69–70, 72, 76
Villa, Pancho, 73, 76, 95

Waco, Texas, 12, 89, 104
Waggoner, Dan, 56
Waggoner, W. T., 4, 56
Walpole's, 83
Ware, Dick, 35, 38
Welsh, Mickey, 78

West Texas, 30, 33, 41, 42–44, 48–49, 50, 52, 53, 60–62, 65–67, 97, 98–106, 111, 115–19, 120
"wild man" (bootlegger), 114–15
windmills, 52, 53, 58, 65, 66, 71, 97, 111
World War I, 101–105
wrangler, 11, 17

XIT Ranch, 52

Z Bar L Ranch, 74, 97, 100
Zuloaga family, 72

www.ingramcontent.com/pod-product-compliance
Lightning Source LLC
Chambersburg PA
CBHW031250290426
44109CB00012B/514